Nuffield College Memories
A Personal History

by
Robert Taylor

Contents

Illustrations

Front cover
6 June 1958, Nuffield College is presented with its Charter.
From left: Sir Norman Chester, Viscount Nuffield, Mayor of Oxford,
Duke of Edinburgh, Earl of Macclesfield (Lord-Lieutenant,
Oxfordshire), Thomas Sherrer Ross Boase (Vice-Chancellor of the
University of Oxford).

Frontispiece
Lord Nuffield

Facing page 32
(clockwise from top left)
AD Lindsay (Leonard Leslie Brooke)
GDH Cole (William Rothenstein)
Norman Chester (David Hockney)
Margery Perham (William Rothenstein)

Facing page 36
Model of the first, rejected, design for the College
Model of the first approved design

Foreword by the Warden

The Charter of Nuffield was brought to the College by the Duke of Edinburgh on 6 June 1958, fifty years ago. Time for a College history, the Fellows thought. Indeed, some past and present members of the College had been thinking about it for a long time. Norman Chester left three unfinished chapters. Chelly Halsey, David Butler and John Darwin had all assembled material and a random selection of past students had been invited to send in their reminiscences. But it was only the imminence of the fiftieth anniversary that spurred us into getting something into print.

We have been fortunate to secure the help of Robert Taylor (Student 1965-68), who is both an experienced journalist and a distinguished historian, to pull things together. What he has produced is not an Official History. Many in the College have helped him and many will not agree with everything he says. But he has written his own uncensored view of the evolution of the College and we are very grateful to him.

He has discovered new facts about the College's early days and for many he will revive poignant memories of their first ventures into scholarship and serious academic life, and of the excitement of helping to shape a quite new college. He has conjured up well-remembered figures from the past – Fellows, Students, and Staff.

This is a story of building, not just in bricks and mortar, but also building traditions, and building an institutional and academic agenda. Indeed one of the striking things about this history is the number of people who are quoted on the subject of what Nuffield ought to be. So I feel quite safe in adding my own opinions to the pot.

First, I know there are lots of things that it can never be, including a business school, a research centre, a school of public policy or government, or, indeed, a monolithic entity of any kind, and quite right too. In fact, it is a small, highly international, College in the University of Oxford, specialising in certain aspects of Social Science. It acts as home for around twenty per cent of the permanent members of the relevant University academic departments and around four per cent of

Oxford Social Science post-graduates. Furthermore, most of its Permanent Fellows are appointed by the University, not by the College.

Despite the small size of the College, it has very strong international academic credibility. It has a higher proportion of Fellows of the British Academy than any other comparable institution in the UK, probably the best group of Social Science post-docs in the world and a bunch of very high quality graduate students. This credibility has been built up over the last fifty years and is a necessary condition for having any lasting impact in the public policy, or indeed any other, arena. This is particularly so if evidence-based policy-making becomes a serious reality.

So, to echo the Introduction, what is the College for? It has to engage with the University and its relevant departments because the Fellows, Post-Docs and Students themselves are so engaged. On top of this, there is an ever-increasing number of departments, groups, centres and institutes within the Social Science Division of the University, some endowed by benefactors. Many of these are headed by, or involve members of the College and, as time goes on, it would be in our interest that these be located in the vicinity of the College. This is not a pipedream because the West End of Oxford, between Nuffield and the Saïd Business School, is going to be redeveloped in the medium term and at least some of it is owned by Nuffield.

Basically, what the College is for is to facilitate the intellectual activities of its members, to enable them to do things, either individually or collectively, which push back the frontiers and help the junior members move up to the frontier. Of course, some are bound to become involved with the wider world because this is what many social scientists like to do once they have established their academic credibility. And luckily, while this activity cannot be subject to central planning, it has the blessing of the College Charter. On top of this, the interaction with the external world which the Visiting Fellowship allows us to maintain is of enormous value to the College in general and particularly to those of the Permanent Fellowship who like to get on the train to London from time to time. Of course, we also hope the Visiting Fellows enjoy our company in return.

So, basically, once we have looked after the students, and made sure the staff are happy, then Nuffield College is there to aid, abet and encourage its Fellows and Post-Docs to do what they like on the research front, not to push them down any particular tracks but to try and ensure that all the available tracks are open.

Stephen J Nickell
March 2008

Annemarie
House
1945

What Are We Here for? Nuffield's Permanent Question

The purposes of Nuffield College have exercised and often baffled the minds of the College's Wardens, Fellows and Students since its foundation three-quarters of a century ago. This is not a philosophical problem. From the very beginning the reasons for Nuffield's existence were not easily and neatly self-evident. But nobody can doubt the College's importance in the development of the social sciences in British higher education since the end of the Second World War. This is a highly personalised history of the College. It deals with many of its personalities and the key events that helped to make Nuffield what it is today. This is not a scholarly exposition or an 'official' history. But, while it seeks to entertain, the book's intention is also to raise serious issues about Nuffield's role in Oxford University, in the social sciences in Britain and overseas and in the world of public policy-making from the middle of the twentieth century.

In 2008 Nuffield is plainly a small but formidable academic institution. You only have to consult the latest directory for 2006-2007 from the British Academy to recognise the College's singular contribution to scholarly endeavour. An estimated third of the economists listed as current Fellows of the British Academy have experienced some direct or indirect connection with Nuffield. Among those categorised by the British Academy as Fellows in political studies, political theory, government and international relations, just under a quarter have or had some similar relationship with the College while that same proportion is apparent among those deemed to be covered by sociology, demography and social statistics. In addition, half a dozen of the Academy's Fellows among the historians are linked in some way today, or have been in the past, with Nuffield. This is an impressive achievement by any measure. It reflects the high level of scholarship that is nurtured within its walls.

The international standing of the College cannot be in dispute. It can boast of three of its past Fellows who have won Nobel Prizes for economics – Sir John Hicks, Sir James Mirrlees and Amartya Sen. Its most eminent alumnus in contemporary political life is Manmohan

Singh, the current Prime Minister of India, who was that country's modernizing Finance Minister during the 1990s. Singh was at Nuffield in the late 1950s where he researched a doctoral thesis on India's export policies and its prospects for self-sustained growth. He was an academic and then Governor of the Reserve Bank of India before going into politics as a prominent member of the Congress party.

The other Prime Minister who passed through Nuffield is Kofi Busia from Ghana. As a Student in the 1940s he wrote a doctoral thesis on *The Position of the Chief in the Modern Political System of Ashanti: A study of the influence of contemporary social changes on Ashanti political institutions*, which was published in 1951. Busia was a close friend of the legendary Margery Perham, who was appointed as Nuffield's first Official Fellow in the autumn of 1939. After the overthrow of Kwame Nkrumah and the return to democratic government in Ghana, Busia was elected Prime Minister in 1969 but he was overthrown by a military coup and died three years later while on a visit to England.

The intellectual renown of individual Fellows of Nuffield or those who spent at least a period of their academic careers in the College is equalled by the wide range of non-academic bodies, including the media, the civil service, the Bank of England, politics and non-governmental organisations, where former Students or Research Fellows were and are employed in senior positions. An Appendix at the end of the book lists some of the published works by existing Fellows of the College. But since the end of the Second World War a steady flow of impressive and lasting volumes have appeared from Nuffield.

A number of other salient facts ought to be made clear from the beginning. The Student intake over the years has been especially striking. Where have they mostly come from? The answer is the Students have arrived increasingly from abroad. Now over half of them did not graduate from British universities before coming to Nuffield. The average proportion of overseas born Students was forty-three per cent between 1945 and 2000. It has been estimated that ten per cent of Nuffield Students came to the College from the United States and a further six per cent from Australia and New Zealand. But increasingly Students from western Europe have found the College an attractive place to be for their research projects. On average they have accounted for eight per cent of all Students over the College's first fifty years but the proportion has risen markedly in recent decades.

What is also revealing is the presence in Nuffield of UK-born students who did not go to a privately-run secondary school. It is true that in the first few decades public schools accounted for just over half the UK-born College student intake but since 1990 the proportion has dropped to no more than a third.

The most impressive feature of the available data on Nuffield Students is the rising importance of women. Until 1980 the average proportion of female Students in the College failed to rise above twenty per cent. But in 2008 over half the Nuffield Student intake are women. There was a startling shift in the gender balance after 1995.

Where did most Nuffield Students go after they left the College? The answer is mainly into academic posts in British universities but the trend has remained uneven. Between 1961 and 1965 the proportion of College Students heading off to academia soared to eighty-seven per cent, reflecting the opening of an increasing number of new Universities and their need for social scientists to populate their recently-created departments. But times have changed. Very few ex-Nuffield students went to work in business up to the early 1990s. But between 1996 and 2000 the proportion rose to as much as twenty-nine per cent and that proportion has gone on increasing as academic posts have grown fewer in number and perhaps less attractive in terms of remuneration and working conditions. In contrast, the lure of lucrative pay and benefits in jobs in the City of London and financial services worldwide has undoubtedly attracted many Nuffield Students, especially in economics. The proportion entering the public services has fluctuated over the years but not as significantly. Fuller details of the origins and destinations of Nuffield Students can be found in the Appendices.

The most startling fact about the history of the College has been its wealth. It is true – as we shall see – that the College suffered a financial problem in 1975. But this was quickly overcome by some limited austerity measures. In 1958 Nuffield's total capital was estimated at just over £1 million. By 2000 the figure was £96 million. Fifty years ago the

College's annual budget amounted to just over £78,000. By 2000 it had risen to £4.7 million.

This book is not an exercise in self-congratulation. Throughout its first seventy years the College was often controversial, envied and despised in equal measure by its innumerable critics, especially in Oxford University. Of course, Nuffield has also had many admirers since its foundation in November 1937, both inside and outside Oxford. But its intellectual journey was never to prove easy. For friends and foes alike the permanent question facing the College has always been 'what is it for?'

'Is Nuffield really a College?' *Oxford Today* asked in its 2001 Trinity term issue. The magazine suggested that a case could be made out for Nuffield as being *'a think tank, an ivory tower, a professional school, a monastery, a kitchen cabinet, a department within a department or an interdisciplinary centre'*. The *Oxford Today* article came to the conclusion that Nuffield was in fact a combination of *'many images – monastery, professional school and adjunct to the corridors of power'*. The result, it suggested, amounted to *'a return to a very old recipe for an Oxford College'*. The questioning nature of the *Oxford Today* article was apt. Nuffield's multiplicity of purposes and roles has been the subject of public debate ever since its controversial inception just over seventy years ago.

Every Oxford College, like any other established institution, is much more than merely the stone, bricks and mortar of its buildings. Nuffield's own history reflects and was shaped by the aspirations and activities of the men and women who were and are its members as permanent Fellows, Post-Doctoral Fellows, Research Fellows and Students. Through the complex and dynamic interaction between the people and the institution to which they belong or passed through emerged a distinctive ethos, tradition and even – although more debatable – a particular collegial personality. In this complex process of interaction between its personalities and institution, Nuffield has been no different from other Colleges in the University. But from its very origins the College was regarded by many in Oxford as an unsettling and even threatening phenomenon.

What was this newly conceived College really for?

4

Nuffield's stated aims as a College were always to be distinctive and varied and they have often been contested and controversial. Its Deed of Covenant and Trust speaks of *'the erection of a College for post-graduate work, especially in connection with the study by co-operation between academic and non-academic persons of social (including economic and political) problems and also for any other post-graduate research or work'*. That key document, written in 1937, goes on to declare that *'the University shall have full power to determine from time to time in its discretion the best method of carrying out such purposes'*. The Schedules attached to The Deed of Covenant and Trust set out in a little more detail what the purposes of the College were envisaged to be.

First of all, it was emphasised that the post-graduate research proposed to take place at Nuffield would be *'especially but not exclusively'* to cover *'the field of social studies'*. It was also determined that the College should ensure there was *'co-operation between academic and non-academic persons'*.

In many important respects – as the Deed of Covenant and Trust indicates – the College was well ahead of its time. The prospect of a wholly residential graduate non-teaching College in Oxford was radical enough for many Fellows of the University in the late 1930s. They believed that Oxford consisted of a complex network of independent autonomous colleges and that they existed essentially as teaching institutions where the country's 'best and brightest' undergraduates were supposed to receive their higher education. In the late 1930s graduate education of any kind hardly existed at all in Britain. Oxford colleges themselves offered few facilities for those who wished to remain in the University to do research after their graduation with an honours degree. Nor did the colleges display much enthusiasm or encouragement for the promotion of post-graduate research. This apparent official attitude of relative indifference persisted even as late as the 1960s and perhaps, in some cases, beyond.

But the innovatory character of the proposed new College was even more pronounced when it came to its particular field of academic study and research. Nuffield was to be a graduate College that was almost exclusively focused on work in the so-called 'social studies'. What might be covered by that all-embracing but ill-defined term in the 1930s was always highly debatable. It certainly seemed to include more than economics, philosophy and politics. Law, history, anthropology and social administration were also regarded as suitably relevant 'modern' subjects for the College to research and study. The decision to restrict entry into Nuffield for Fellows and Research Students broadly to those subjects alone was a matter of some fierce contention. It is worth noting that the original Deed of Covenant and Trust seemed to leave open the possibility that the College would 'not exclusively' be concerned with social studies. Some Fellows in other Oxford Colleges such as the medieval historian, Sir Maurice Powicke, even expressed a wish that the proposed graduate College might cover medieval historical topics. There were also those who wanted to see the study and research of English literature and other subjects in the humanities in general carried out at Nuffield. Such suggestions failed to win much approval from the University authorities but they reflected an undercurrent of doubt and scepticism among some academics about the seriousness of social studies as a rigorous subject for scholarly research in one focused graduate College.

The insistence, contained in both the Deed of Covenant and Trust as well as in Nuffield's Statutes that the proposed College should ensure co-operation in research between academic and non-academic persons was equally the focus of some controversy and perhaps it always has been. The College's Founder Lord Nuffield and A D Lindsay, then the University Vice-Chancellor as well as Master of Balliol College, were both determined that the College should be allowed to develop as an educational institution which would devote itself to the development and encouragement of a common and co-operative collaboration that was designed somehow to integrate academia with the outside world of the public policy makers. They envisaged Nuffield as a graduate College that could help to break down what they saw as the existing walls that separated academic scholarship from the realities of every day life or the wider society of politics, business and finance. Social studies, Lindsay at least believed, would help to encourage the creation of a common ground where academic theory would somehow be linked to practical action in dealing with contemporary social and economic problems. Whatever different forms such co-operation might take, it was implied, would be achieved through trial and error. The initial proposal for the appointment of up to twenty non-academic outsiders as Visiting Fellows, who were to be people of recognised power and influence in public administration and politics, business and the trade unions, was always seen as crucial for the purposes of the College. It was believed their presence at Nuffield would bring a distinctive quality to what it was trying to do.

In addition, it was proposed from the outset that the College was to open its doors to both men and women on more or less equal terms. The Statutes explained that women were to be *'eligible for Fellowships and Studentships'* in Nuffield although it added hastily that of course they would *'not be permitted to reside in the College'*. The very suggestion that both sexes might be able to join the new College aroused obvious misgivings in 1930s Oxford, especially if men and women were not going to enjoy equal rights when it came to residential accommodation. The radical nature of the concept of gender equality – pressed in particular by Lindsay – should be judged by the fact that even St Antony's College did not permit women as full students until as late as 1962. But, as we shall see, Nuffield didn't live up to that early promise of gender equality in practice for some time, at least among its Fellows up until the present day and until quite recently among its Student intake.

This short book seeks to provide a broad and personal portrait of the evolution of Nuffield College since its beginnings in 1937 as it seems to this author. It does not claim to be a comprehensive history. Nor is it an official history. I have been granted freedom in my researches. The end result is entirely my own responsibility. This book seeks to examine, however, just how far it has been possible for the College to remain true to the ambitious and idealistic hopes and aspirations of its founders and Statutes. Inevitably Nuffield needed to compromise and accommodate, at least in finding a place for itself in Oxford University as well as in the wider society and political economy. In the culture and traditions of one of the oldest Universities in the world, this was necessary and perhaps inevitable. In the agreement to have a Chapel at Nuffield, a Coat of Arms and all the revered protocols of the older Colleges like Latin prayers at High Table and a well-stocked wine cellar, Nuffield acknowledged its need to reassure the rest of the University that it was not envisaged as some kind of subversive threat to the settled, existing order. On the contrary its founders were keen to prove that Nuffield was ready to fit in to what others expected of an Oxford College, even if its intake were to devote their time exclusively to the study of the modern world. There was never to be a Grand Plan for the College. But over time it was able to establish its own distinctive personality although this has always been flexible and ambiguous enough to have changed in many profound ways during its first seventy years of life.

It is important to recognise from the outset that there was nothing like Nuffield in 1937 in British higher education. Even today the College still remains a rather distinctive, and some would say, peculiar institution. Other centres of higher learning were created in 'modern' studies in Oxford after the Second World War. The Oxford Management Centre at Templeton College and the Saïd Business School both reflected the emergence of new demands for graduate work in 'modern' studies in Oxford. The creation of potentially strong and separate Departments of Economics, Politics and International Relations and Sociology at the end of the 1990s has clearly strengthened the institutional presence of those subjects outside the framework of the College. But Nuffield never sought to develop in ways that would have made such developments unnecessary or of secondary importance. Some College Fellows and former Students would have liked Nuffield to grow and become in effect the more or less exclusive centre of social studies in the University by expanding its intake of Fellows and Students. Others regretted that the College did not turn itself into a Harvard Business School or a Massachusetts Institute of Technology, let alone a Brookings Institution. Others believe the College missed its way because it never established a Kennedy School of Government as at Harvard University within its wall when it might have done. Nuffield refused to emulate nor was it influenced by the experience of graduate or public policy making institutions in other parts of the advanced western world. The College stood at a distance from such developments in its own autonomous independence or some would say it remained in a somewhat surly or arrogant isolation for far too long. It would be wrong to suggest, that as a result Nuffield suffered from anything as melodramatic as a crisis of identity, let alone one of purpose. There was, however, an ambivalence about the College and no settled view about its ultimate purposes. Nor was it determined whether they were compatible with one another, let alone achievable.

Except for a brief period of financial difficulty that hit Nuffield during the mid 1970s due to the plummeting stock market after the quadrupling of oil prices during and after the Yom Kippur war, the College has become one of the richest in Oxford University. This was not due to the generosity of the Founder once his initial endowment had been spent on the building of the College. Nor did Nuffield's wealth stem in later years from property or further benefactions, or even from successful alumni but rather from the returns of a shrewd investment strategy on the stock market. But even in its specific academic ethos Nuffield was somehow able to survive and prosper without the need to resort to any fundamental re-appraisal or revision of its original purposes, as set out in the College's 1937 Deed of Covenant and Trust.

As this book will argue, however, during its first seventy years Nuffield did evolve and not always in ways that its founders might have envisaged. It was born in hard times. Britain was recovering slowly from the ravages of the Great Depression. Mass unemployment and poverty remained visible social evils, especially in the assisted regions of northern England, Scotland and South Wales. It is true much of southern England, including Oxford itself, was starting to enjoy some of the fruits of material prosperity. But there were few signs of much fresh thought going into economic and social policy-making in government circles on what to do about contemporary domestic problems like mass unemployment and chronic poverty and ill health. Higher education in Britain was still mostly confined to a socially exclusive ruling elite, drawn from a privileged upper class. Modern or social studies were not regarded as serious academic pursuits by most

University teachers. Field-work or the use of quantitative social surveys were hard to find. The nearest to such work was perhaps only visible in Tom Harrison's impressionistic and subjective Mass Observation studies of public opinion. The 1930s in Britain were a relatively bleak age for social experimentation and risk-taking in academia as everywhere else. As Chelly Halsey, College Fellow in Sociology, argued in his 1994 David Glass memorial lecture;

> '*Between the wars before the social sciences became established ...*
> *knowledge of both government and governed was essentially amateur,*
> *a wisdom ascribed to politicians and civil servants. Only occasionally*
> *would some academic mandarin such as Keynes, or Beveridge,*
> *influence Westminster, Whitehall and public opinion. For the most*
> *part practical men picked up their sociology, economics and politics*
> *from experience, the Bible, and classical allusion.'*

This general situation in Britain towards the end of the 1930s makes it all the more commendable that Oxford University gave the go-ahead for the creation of Nuffield College in the particular way that Lindsay envisaged.

During the Second World War and in its immediate aftermath, Nuffield was regarded by many admiring outsiders and perhaps even by some of its own Fellows as a crucial institution for the building of the new world – rational, civilised, egalitarian perhaps or at least paternalistic and committed to research projects that might help to conquer poverty through the benevolent power of a paternalistic state. It might also work for the rights and obligations of what the sociologist T H Marshall famously defined at the time as 'social citizenship'. It is not hard to understand why the College was seen as an integral part of that broad Middle Way of the so-called post-war social settlement.

But from the start Nuffield always regarded itself as an uncompromisingly elitist and meritocratic institution which was dedicated to the furtherance of high academic standards in all its scholarly activities. Critics might suggest the social sciences attracted the weakest students. But the College was always determined to refute such prejudice and ignorance. Under Norman Chester as Warden it might have seemed to some in Oxford that the College was an unwelcome and awkward interloper from the gritty north, a Mancunian establishment that, despite its adherence to the trappings of Oxford's rituals and traditions, was perhaps a gauche and awkward addition to the University. Of course, the University in Nuffield's early years was hardly *Brideshead Revisited*. In the 1940s and 1950s it established an international reputation for itself as being formidably competitive and earnest. Oxford was seen as a place where clever boys and girls, who benefited from the advantages of passing the selective eleven-plus examination by going to state grammar schools, came to study. Alan Bennett's recent play, *The History Boys*, is an invocation of that lost world of working-class aspiration. In the all-too-brief age when the distribution of wealth and income in Britain began to narrow and converge after 1945, Nuffield was often portrayed as a crucial part of what seemed like a progressive age of opportunity and social mobility.

We shall see in this book that the College did not travel up and up effortlessly on a kind of teleological journey to some social science utopia or social democratic idyll. There is no Whig version of Nuffield history to be written. If I use the term 'golden age' to describe the time of Norman Chester's years as College Warden, I have felt the need to place it in inverted commas. But as the many fond memories conveyed by Nuffield alumni to the questionnaire sent out by David Butler in 2006-2007 indicate, their time at the College in those years from the 1950s to the 1970s is still seen by many of its former Students as an important and often one of the most influential and formative periods of their lives. The distinguished careers of so many of them in public affairs and academia not just in Britain but across the world is impressive by any standards and testifies to the College's attractions and its ability to select from strong competition among the best and brightest of each generation in modern studies.

The success or failure of the College over its first seventy years needs, however, to be assessed against the changing nature of the outside world in which it existed and developed. Britain abandoned gradually many of the assumptions and aspirations of the post-war period. The country grew more individualistic, more fragmented and increasingly hostile to the moral and social values and traditions that had helped to form and shape Britain after 1945. Nuffield, like almost every other institution, failed to forecast the arrival of those new times. The College was never to become a centre for neo-liberalism, let alone Thatcherism. It found it difficult, even if it was perhaps never willing to admit this to itself, to adjust to what were more unpredictable and unstable outside circumstances in society and the economy. Inevitably something was lost in the life of the College as a result. But it would be wrong to exaggerate the abruptness of the changes that occurred in Nuffield after the 1970s. There was always to be more continuity than change as perhaps many admirers of the 'golden age' were not prepared to admit – not least in the expansion of a more sophisticated empiricism in what became the three almost exclusively dominant subject streams in the College; economics, politics and sociology. Nuffield appeared to grow more selective in its academic pursuits and narrowed down their focus as the core areas were reinforced through a process of self-selection in the hardening Group system of academic organisation in the College. In doing this the College seemed, on the face of it, to grow less relevant to the public policy-makers than it had used to be. However, the fault for such a trend lay on both sides. At the same time, the College moved consciously more boldly outwards into the wider world of international scholarship where it was able to achieve a deserved fame and reputation in the social sciences across Europe, the United States and much further afield, especially under Wardens Sir David Cox and Sir Tony Atkinson. As a result of those new difficult times Nuffield began to find a modern role for itself which in some ways was markedly different on balance from that which had been originally envisaged by the College founders. To some observers this might have become a matter of regret. But there is no need for any resort to nostalgia or myth-making in our understanding of the College's tangled, complex history. There may have been no single person after Norman Chester who could provide a clear and credible strategy that was able to transform Nuffield completely into a modern institution for higher learning in the social sciences that at least was at ease with itself. The reconciliation of the College's original purposes with the demands placed upon it by the realities and aspirations of the post-industrial age of mass higher education and internationalisation was never going to be easy. Moreover, Nuffield was also forced to come to terms with the greater technical sophistication in skills and knowledge that were required in the social sciences, although it is worth emphasising that many of its more adventurous Fellows were always enthusiastic pioneers in that important development. In this, the College came to acknowledge, at least implicitly, that it was no longer possible to attempt to bridge the gulf between academia and the world of 'practical' men which had so concerned Lord Nuffield and Lindsay in the 1930s. In fact, the gap they worried about then has grown into a yawning chasm over the past seventy years. However, there may be some signs of a shift back in the College to a greater awareness of the need for contemporary relevance. Some important connections can be found in the College today that suggest efforts are underway to try and re-establish a kind of reconciliation between its core social science research interests and the demands of the outside world. There is no need for any rupture of current practice. Nor do we need to question first principles. The Age of Change is a constant fact in the lives of all human beings and it has been since the beginning of history. As Norman Chester said in a preface to a lecture on Nuffield's purposes he gave on 10 June 1978 just before his retirement as Warden;

> 'In a small institution (like Nuffield) comparatively small shifts of emphasis may, over a period, change the main course of its contribution. Only by returning from time to time to the main purpose can the institution be kept on course'.

The central focus of this book is concerned with trying to examine the crucial question of what Nuffield College was and is for. In that 1978 talk Chester also said;

> 'Those who guide institutions should have clearly in mind the purpose which the institution is required to fulfil. And, any assessment of the success or failure of an institution must be measured by the degree of its success in fulfilling its purpose.'

His wise words have provided me with a guiding light and the central theme for my own highly personal journey through the College's fascinating history – from A D Lindsay under the gathering clouds of a

European war to Warden Steve Nickell in a no less turbulent and menacing world. The resolution of social and economic problems through the use of objective and measurable social data, rational and independent discussion and empirical observation, remains as important to Nuffield in 2008 as it did in 1937.

In concluding thoughts I will offer some tentative but practical suggestions on how Nuffield might develop in the years ahead without any need for the College to abandon either its current pursuits or what still remains of its original purposes. 'Back to the Future' may have become an unfashionable maxim in an age that despises or forgets the history of even its contemporary past. As a modern historian myself but one who spent most of his working life in journalism, mainly at the *Observer* and the *Financial Times* but also at the now sadly long gone social science weekly *New Society* covering mostly industrial relations, labour markets and British politics, I remain unrepentant in my conviction that contemporary history should lie at the core of 'modern' studies. One of the pleasures of researching this short book over the past twelve months has been to recognise and be reminded constantly of the admirably high standards and prolific nature of the history writing that has come both from Fellows and former Students of the College over the years. Many at Nuffield today might frown and curse history but it has often managed to infiltrate some of their own research work as well. It surprises me continually that the assertion that history is important for our understanding of today's world has to be made at all. I remain convinced, however, that the social sciences can best thrive if they are aware of the past and that of the societies they dissect and assess by an analysis of current data no matter how sophisticated the techniques. The varieties of contemporary capitalism cannot really be understood, for example, without a sober recognition of the uneven and unpredictable histories of different societies and countries. Our modern world is not a *tabula rasa* for social or political experimentation. It comes from a tangled and complex past, only a small part of which we can fully understand.

This introduction provides me with the opportunity to write just a few words on my own years in the College. I was a Student at Nuffield from September 1965 until September 1968, when I moved to become a lecturer in the history department of what was then the new University of Lancaster. My first class honours degree in Oxford was in modern history and not politics, philosophy and economics. This was not an apparent problem, however, in securing a studentship at the College at that time. I was much influenced in my application to come to Nuffield by Pat Thompson, my tutor in nineteenth-century history at Wadham and Hugh Clegg, then one of Nuffield's most influential Fellows. The eventual subject for my thesis was unashamedly political history – Lord Randolph Churchill and Tory Democracy in the 1880s. It reflected what has turned into a lifetime interest and what still remains a relatively unexplored and under-researched social as well as political problem, namely why a substantial part of the British working classes voted in a parliamentary democracy for the Conservatives – the party of the right – from the Second Reform Act of 1867 until the last decade of the twentieth century. A short biography of the 3rd Marquess of Salisbury was the offshoot of my unfinished research work and it was published in 1975 when I was immersed as a correspondent in the turbulent industrial events of that decade.

I found – like many other students of my generation – that the College was a wonderful place to be at a time when graduate students in Oxford University were still finding it difficult to secure much attention and interest from the undergraduate Colleges. Nuffield was a symbol of relative material affluence. Its standard of living for Students was quite exceptional. It was like residing in a four-star hotel by the standards of the 1960s. But the College was also highly intensive and competitive in argument and debate – from the breakfast table to after dinner coffee. Nuffield was a strong believer and diligent practitioner of the work ethic and there was little time for any small talk. To outsiders then and probably now Nuffield was always a source of envy and resentment. It was seen by many as rather arrogant and stand-offish and it was disliked by those in the University who were dismissive of the growing importance of the social sciences and regarded Nuffield as a subversive threat or at least a barbaric intrusion into the settled Oxford way of life.

However, for my part I always found Nuffield stimulating and challenging. It was a time when its Student body was polarised on increasingly ideological lines. The College became briefly a centre of student revolutionary activity in Oxford but it also contained some delightful old Fogeyish elements. Disputes even carried on over the breakfast bacon and eggs. In May 1968 I and a number of the more middle of the road Students decided to travel to Paris to witness *Les Evénements*. The *enragé* in the College showed little interest in leaving its comfortable confines to see what was happening in France for themselves. They seemed to prefer sitting in deck chairs round the College pond, not mounting the barricades at the Sorbonne and Nanterre University. I hasten to add that those Paris travellers from Nuffield did not mount the barricades either but listened to anarchists declaiming in the Odéon theatre and students in the quadrangle of the Sorbonne arguing over which sectarian group of the ultra-left they should join. This author recalls a visit we made to the worker-occupied Renault factory at Billancourt in the outskirts of Paris where we were told to f--- off in French and walking through the lengthening grass across the normally manicured lawns of the Palace of Versailles where the gardeners had also gone on strike.

My student years in the College covered the transition from optimism to pessimism in the prevailing attitudes to Harold Wilson's modernising Labour government and perhaps – though we did not know it at the time – the beginning of the final years of what became known as the age of the so-called social settlement that was said to have dominated mainstream British politics and society since the end of the Second World War. The vaguely implicit Social Democratic project – of which Nuffield seemed then to be an integral part – was coming under relentless outside stress from both left and right. As a result it was starting to disintegrate, if only slowly. In the late 1960s it often still seemed that most College Fellows, especially Nuffield's economists, were travelling every weekday on the 8.55 morning train to London to advise and influence Labour government ministers. For their part, eminent senior Labour ministers like George Brown, Jim Callaghan, Tony Crosland, Shirley Williams and Tony Benn were conspicuous by their presence in the College from time to time. It all seemed to confirm my Wordsworthian feelings of the moment – that Bliss it was to be alive but to be young and in Nuffield was very Heaven.

This book is concerned almost exclusively with the College Fellows and Students, with the events, researches and discussions that they were involved in during their time at Nuffield. But I want to take this opportunity to acknowledge the indispensable role of the College support staff in making Nuffield at all possible as a successful, working institution – the cleaners, the kitchen staff, the librarians, the secretaries, the cooks, the porters, the administrators and the research officers and assistants. Many of them devoted most of their working lives in loyal service to the College. We should remember and honour them because they are also indispensable to our understanding of Nuffield's history. The material comforts of the College are much commented upon in the memories of former Students which are related in this book. It is therefore a pity that only one of them – George Jones, who has recently retired from being Professor of Government at the London School of Economics and Political Science – actually mentioned the crucial role that the support staff played in the story of the College. Perhaps he did so because, like this author, he married one of Nuffield's admirable secretaries. Without the staff's selfless dedication Nuffield would not have advanced over the years in the way that it has done and this should never be forgotten.

A good example of that loyal service to the College can be found in the story of Audrey Skeats who worked as a Secretary at Nuffield for forty-five years, from 1951 until her retirement in June 1996. Her vivid memories of her time in the College, conveyed in her farewell speech, provide us with her own personal reflections of how Nuffield had changed in her perspective over that eventful period:

> 'In 1950 I had an interview with the then Warden Mr Loveday and he said 'Well you're a bit young for what we want but we'll see how you get on.' So I started here and was given three Fellows to work for. One was called David Butler. He had just been made a Research Fellow and I thought 'H'm I could have been given an Official Fellow!' Anyway as it happened we worked together for most of the next forty years. One of the other

Fellows was Sir Donald MacDougall, the economist who is now an Honorary Fellow of the College.

In the early 1950s there was not much of the College built. We were all squeezed into nearly three staircases. You entered the College from New Road through mud and chicken wire. Secretary's lives then were a bit different than they are now. The Warden's secretary ruled. She would come into our room and say 'One of the Visiting Fellows is coming down this weekend to dictate his book. Any volunteers? Right we'll have you Audrey this Sunday and I'd be taking shorthand for hours on end to the musical accompaniment of the thump thump of the pile drivers laying down the foundations of the unbuilt staircases – added to this was the billowing smoke from Herbert Morrison's pipe.

In 1969 I started to work for John Goldthorpe and he introduced me to sociology. For the first time I did not understand what I was typing but eventually I learned some of the language. Working for Freddie Madden, the historian of the British Commonwealth, I didn't have that problem as he wrote – for me – in a more understandable vocabulary.

1982 saw the birth of the international journal – Electoral Studies *– and I have seen that grow over the last fifteen years. It will take some time before I can relax when I hear an election has been announced in say Papua New Guinea and not to have to worry about who is going to write the Election Note.*

Thank goodness that in the 1980s I was introduced to word processors. Although I must say they weren't my sentiments at the time for I used to lose more work than I saved.

The 1990s have seen Iain McLean doing his best to turn me into an electronic robot. He has almost managed it as I am now beginning to get impatient with people who haven't got http://www addresses, let alone e-mail ones. So before I get entangled in the World Wide Web I am going to escape – back into the snail mail world'.

Other long serving College staff should be remembered as well. Christine Kennedy was Librarian for thirty-four years from 1961 to 1994. She made the Library a joy to work in with her tolerance, enthusiasm, interest and understanding. Jean Brotherhood was the College's chief secretary for thirty-six years from 1953 to 1989. The chef for nearly thirty years was Ken Hudson, from 1958 until 1987 while Gerry Smith was the butler from 1962 until 1984. The College handyman, Charlie Wheeler, was also a loyal College staff member for many years as was Tom Cross, the rather grand Head Porter.

It was a pleasure to be given this assignment in June 2007 to write a short, personal history of Nuffield College for the commemoration of the delivery of its Royal Charter by the Duke of Edinburgh on 6 June 1958. I must thank the current Warden, Steve Nickell, for giving the go-ahead to the project. Other invaluable assistance came from within the College, in particular from Senior Fellow Laurence Whitehead, sociologists John Goldthorpe and Chelly Halsey as well as imperial historian John Darwin and Desmond King, Mellon Professor of American Government. Sir Brian Harrison was very helpful and I appreciate his kindness in letting me use the verbatim notes of interviews he conducted with a number of Fellows of the College in recent times. Special thanks must be given especially to David Butler who played an active role in seeing this book through to completion

Many of today's Nuffield support staff were important in the production of this book. I am particularly grateful to Justine Crump, Clare Kavanagh, Catherine McNeill and Stephanie Wright for helping me with their efficiency, courtesy and often a necessary understanding of how to find a way through the often frustrating intricacies of the College bureaucracy. Nuffield is no different to other institutions nowadays in the way it is administered. Countless Students that I met during my brief stays at the College over 2007-2008 have provided me with personal insights and views about Nuffield as it is today and they have helped me to achieve what I hope is a reasonable sense of perspective and balance.

This book was constructed on the strong foundations that were first laid down by both David Butler and Chelly Halsey in their own uncompleted researches into the College's history. An unfinished draft of the origins of Nuffield written by Norman Chester was important as well. Five recorded seminars were carried out in the College over 2006-

2007 on relevant topics in Nuffield's history. These covered the three subject areas, economics, politics and sociology, as well as the views and memories of the last three living Wardens – Michael Brock, Sir David Cox and Sir Tony Atkinson. An important session was also held on the College's finances when many of the surviving domestic Bursars reminisced on how they turned Nuffield into one of the richest Colleges in Oxford University. The transcripts of those sessions were particularly useful in the preparation of this monograph. I am especially thankful for a written paper presented to the College's economics group by Christopher Bliss. This provided me with many insights into the distinguished economists who came to Nuffield.

I also consulted a number of useful primary archives. In the College I found a wealth of material for the early years in the Library although little has apparently been collected for the period since 1978. The papers of A D Lindsay at Keele University provided me with some insights into his enormous influence over the inception of the College. Material contained in Professor Michael Oakeshott's papers deposited in the LSE library in London was of some interest as well. The papers of G D H Cole, Harold Butler and Philip Williams are contained in the College Library and they were also useful.

Much of what I have written owes an immense debt of gratitude to the many former Nuffield Students who kindly conveyed their often colourful and insightful memories and thoughts on their years at the College to a questionnaire sent out by David Butler. A number of Visiting Fellows also provided me with interesting and incisive thoughts on their more recent experiences in the College and on how Nuffield can improve its relationships with the non academic world in the future.

The Making of the College in Peace and War

A D Lindsay's Grand Vision

Lord Nuffield originally wanted to fund the creation of a new post-graduate residential College in Oxford, which would be devoted exclusively to the study of engineering and accountancy. This is what he proposed at his meeting in London on 8 July 1937 with Lord Halifax, the University's Chancellor and also then Lord President of the Council in the Chamberlain government. Lord Nuffield told Lord Halifax that he *'had been much impressed with what seemed to him to be the gap in the equipment of Oxford in engineering and he felt the University compared very unfavourably with Cambridge'*. As a result, he maintained the University had *'lost many good men'*. Lord Nuffield was also concerned with another gap that he believed existed between *'the world of theoretical engineers and the practical men employed in the engineering industry'*. His original vision was of a residential College in Oxford that would bring them both together with well-equipped laboratories and workshops. In addition, Lord Nuffield also wanted his proposed College to focus on the development of modern business studies and in particular on accountancy. He informed Lord Halifax that he was prepared to endow the new College with £900,000 of the fortune he had made from producing cars. The College was to be built on the wharf site, which he had recently purchased for £100,000, on the north side of New Road in the western approaches to the City centre, between Worcester and Pembroke colleges. Lord Nuffield said his primary wish was to improve the rundown western approaches to Carfax and the High Street.

It was clear from the beginning that while Lord Nuffield's proposal for a residential College provided further evidence of his generous financial benevolence to the University, his envisaged primary purpose for the College did not meet with the approval of the senior University authorities. Neither A D Lindsay, the Vice-Chancellor and Master of Balliol College nor Douglas Veale, the University Registrar wanted to see the creation of a post-graduate residential College that was focused exclusively on engineering and business studies such as accountancy. Veale told Lord Nuffield in Oxford on the day after his meeting with Lord Halifax that the University authorities had no wish to duplicate the resources that were already available in engineering at Cambridge. Instead, at Lindsay's instigation, Veale suggested that the proposed College would be more acceptable to the University if it were devoted exclusively to research into modern or social studies. But at the same time the Registrar assured Lord Nuffield that the University welcomed his additional offer of providing £100,000 for the construction of a physical chemical laboratory.

There is no doubt that Lord Nuffield's proposal for a new College in Oxford came at an opportune moment for the University. As one of the founders of the honours school of philosophy, politics and economics established in 1920 and which began awarding honours degrees in 1923, Lindsay had been anxious for some time to further developments in those 'modern' subjects against the often open hostility or at best deep scepticism of the University authorities. Moves were already being made before Lord Nuffield's meeting in London with Lord Halifax to give a boost to social studies. In 1935 the Rockefeller Foundation in the United States agreed to make an annual grant of £5,000 for five years towards research in that subject area at Oxford. It was Lindsay, as Chairman of the University's social studies research committee, who was busily administering that funding source. The recent creation of the Institute of Statistics as well as the Institute of Experimental Psychology in the University also reflected the growing if fragmented and sporadic interest in 'modern' subjects that was emerging in Oxford during the 1930s. In addition, Barnett House – founded in 1913 to train social workers – was carrying out a survey of social services in Oxford and the surrounding area. A study group was also at work examining advisory bodies in their relations with government, while economists were examining the factors that explained the fluctuations in Britain's business activity. Lord Nuffield's unexpected and generous offer to fund the building of a residential College therefore appeared to provide the opportunity for bringing some coherence to those disparate activities and advancing the cause of social studies in Oxford.

On 15 July 1937, Lindsay discussed his vision of what the proposed College might be like with the recently appointed Master of University College, Sir William Beveridge. Surprisingly, Beveridge was less than enthusiastic about the creation of an Oxford College with *'the special aim of developing the study of the conditions and problems of contemporary human society and of bringing members of the University into personal contact with men of affairs'*. *'Is there a case for a new foundation such as that of Keble in the middle of the nineteenth century?'* Beveridge wondered. *'My tentative answer to this would be in the negative and the new institution would be far more valuable if it took another form'*. Beveridge argued that Keble College had *'met a real need of its time, in making collegiate life possible to men of restricted means'*. But he believed this was a less important issue now than it had been then. He pointed out that Oxford Colleges operated a scholarship system and the University had grown *'more democratic generally'*. Nor did Beveridge think it was sensible for the proposed College to focus exclusively on research in social studies.

Lindsay was not persuaded by Beveridge's arguments. He set out his own initial ideas for the proposed College in a paper that he circulated to University colleagues in July 1937. In one extremely important respect he agreed with Lord Nuffield's opinion – that the existing 'gap' between the academic theoreticians and practical men was 'damaging' and needed to be closed and this should be done through the creation of the proposed new College. *'Their co-operation is too sporadic and too formal'*, he argued. *'Men have to know each other before their co-operation becomes really fruitful'*. Much might be achieved, he believed, *'by using the opportunities for intimate talk, discussion and common understanding which an Oxford college can give. The coping stone of the scheme which we have been trying to work out would be a college of post graduate studies, especially devoted to the facts and problems of contemporary society'*.

Lindsay's own conception of the College was certainly ambitious. He envisaged that its Warden would be a *'university man who had plenty of practical experience and knowledge of affairs with the gift of making people work together'*. Lindsay saw the need for the appointment of three different kinds of Fellow in the new College. There would be two or three directors of studies along with six to twelve further research Fellows *'in the study of modern society not covered by the ordinary teacher'* with about ten to twenty additional non-university men of affairs drawn from business, the civil service and local government. They would all have equal rights with each other in the governance of the College with access to rooms and meals. He envisaged the non-university men coming to the College at weekends to take part in discussions on contemporary issues. In addition, the College would have ten to twenty-three junior research Fellows for those who had taken their first honours degrees and had decided to pursue definite pieces of research on the modern world.

It was made clear from the outset that the proposed new College would have to remain firmly under the control of the University authorities. This was unlike any other College in Oxford. Nuffield – Lindsay wrote – was to be *'the University's instrument of research into the facts and problems of contemporary society and its endowments would be the property of the University with its staff directly appointed by the University'*. Lindsay envisaged that Fellows in social studies would be members of the new College but they would also remain attached to their existing Colleges. It was not until 1958, when Nuffield was honoured with the Royal Charter, that the University relinquished its direct authority over the College. For its first twenty-nine years the College was ultimately run by the University as a whole for good and ill.

In a broadcast on the BBC external services on 20 October 1937 Lindsay stressed the new College's overseas importance, especially for the British Dominions. This was an early sign of the international perspective he always had in mind for Nuffield as a post-graduate College in the English-speaking world. Lindsay was also keen to emphasise that the College's intention was to bridge the gulf between academia and the world of public policy-making in the study of the modern world:

'The University has a long tradition of training men to play their part in government, in political life, in the higher reaches of the civil service and in the civil service of India and Africa'

he pointed out.

Lord Nuffield was persuaded to accept Lindsay's arguments for the proposed College's primary purposes. The Founder explained this more fully in the formal proposal that was presented under his name to the University's governing body – the Hebdomadal Council on 8 October 1937 for its approval;

'In the meeting of the demands for new knowledge in the non-scientific subjects there is an ever greater lag than in scientific subjects between research and its practical application. This is in some respects comparable with the separation between the clinical and the laboratory aspects of medical science which recent developments in Oxford are designed to bridge. Struck by this analogy I have been wondering during the past year whether there is any way to bridge the separation between the theoretical students of contemporary civilisation and the men responsible for carrying it on; between the economist, the political theorist, the student of government and administration on the one hand and on the other hand the business man, the politician, the civil servant and the local government official, not to mention the ordinary every day man and woman'.

There was another important feature of the proposed College that aroused some initial anxiety among the University authorities. Lindsay insisted that the College must be open to women as well as men. By the standards of Oxford in 1937 such a suggestion of gender equality between students was nothing short of revolutionary. Lindsay was told bluntly that women posed a great difficulty for the College's development. It was pointed out to him that you could hardly have both sexes living together and if you appropriated a wing to women you would tie yourself down to having as many women Fellows as would fill it. He was advised that it would be best from the start to assume that no women would in fact be resident but without saying anything about it to anybody. It was suggested that an area in the

College building plans should be left free where a women's wing might be erected later on without any fuss. It was eventually agreed after much agonising in the College Statutes that while women would be eligible to become Fellows and students they were not to be allowed to actually live in the College. But Lindsay envisaged that the proposed college would welcome both women as well as men.

He also believed that other existing institutions in the University such as the Institute of Statistics, the Extra Mural Delegacy and Barnett House would be either eventually attached or even absorbed by the College. Although he never suggested openly that Nuffield might become the centre of a cluster of bodies dedicated to 'modern' studies, this was clearly in his mind. In fact, nothing was to come of that particular ambition.

Lindsay's overall concept of what he called *'a new experiment'* in the University was certainly bold and ambitious by the Oxford University standards of the time. He himself acknowledged that *'there had never been anything quite like it before'*. Perhaps nobody else in 1937 in Oxford could have envisaged such an institution. Lindsay believed the creation of Nuffield College would be of profound importance for the future development of the social sciences in Britain. He argued that Oxford's peculiar institutional structure of independent Colleges was ideally suited to advance the creation of a community of scholars and practical men to pursue research and resolve contemporary problems. Now Nuffield would be putting the *'very old institution'* of the Oxford college to a contemporary use.

Some of Oxford University's economists were not so enthusiastic about Lindsay's broad conception of the College. Sir Roy Harrod, then economics Fellow at Christ Church suggested that the Master of Balliol College was not sufficiently sensitive to the needs of economics. He thought that Lindsay believed economics was *'mainly a matter of common sense'* and *'of people getting together and discussing things with mutual good will'*. Harrod and some of his academic economist colleagues thought Lindsay had *'laid too much stress on the College sponsoring large conferences and being a centre of good fellowship'* and that he did *'not appreciate what should be done in relation to the progress of economics considered as a science'*.

Nuffield was *'created at a critical time in the development of Oxford economics'*, Harrod later recorded. *'Econometrics was starting up and some of us thought that Oxford should play a large part in that field. That would entail the right kind of library set-up and research assistance. I do not think that Lindsay consulted the economists at all. He was wilful and headstrong and stuck to his own ideas'*. Harrod would have actually preferred that Nuffield should become an exclusive research College for economists alone. Thankfully this view did not prevail.

But as Christopher Bliss, an emeritus economics Fellow in Nuffield today explained in an unpublished paper on economics in the College in 2007: *'When Nuffield opened its doors it did so as a graduate College in a University without any specialist undergraduate economics degree'*. Bliss argued that it was *'paradoxically Oxford's relative 'backwardness' that facilitated the creation of Nuffield College. The promotion of graduate training was seen in part as making good the limitations of the PPE course. In Cambridge the foundation of graduate Colleges had to wait until 1960s and nothing like Nuffield was ever created or even contemplated. The design of the College showed the effects of its environment with an almost non-existent department. The College provided a partial substitute for a standard department by offering a home to numerous university professors or lecturers, the choice of whom it influenced. In addition, by appointing its own Official Fellows it had a profound effect on Oxford economics, similar to that which might have been made by a departmental head had such existed'*.

However, unlike the other defined social studies, economics in Britain during the 1930s was going through a fertile period of thought, partly explained by the growing influence of J M Keynes. But as Bliss has explained, the condition of economics at that time could only be appreciated by understanding how much remained to be done and by today's standards how *'crude and unfinished'* much of economic theory still remained. He pointed to *'the unsubtle treatment of human behaviour'* by academic economists and their neglect of *'agency'* as well as the underdeveloped nature of international economics.

It is unfortunate that Lindsay himself decided not to become the College's first Warden. He was offered the post but on reflection and with reluctance he turned it down in February 1938. If Lindsay had taken on that task as Warden he could have shaped the College very much in the way that he had envisaged. He was not always so reluctant to try and translate his fertile ideas into practice. In 1949 on his retirement as Master of Balliol College, Lindsay agreed to become the first principal of the newly formed University College of North Staffordshire – later to become the University of Keele. This was very much his own personal creation in the realisation of a long time commitment to the creation of a common curriculum that moulded arts and science subjects together. Nonetheless, between 1938 and his departure from Oxford eleven years later, Lindsay was indirectly but closely involved in the evolution of the Nuffield College project. However, it would certainly have been more sensible for its satisfactory progress if he had been ready to take on the burdens of being Warden from the very beginning.

On the other hand, the existing evidence does not suggest Lindsay had really thought through in much detail the practical implications of what he envisaged Nuffield would be like. Social Studies had advanced only modestly in British higher education during the 1930s. It hardly existed at all as a recognised area for teaching and research outside the confines of the London School of Economics and Political Science. The growth of politics as an academic subject was in particular painfully slow during the early years of the College. *'The Oxford reformists G D H Cole, the Socialist polymath and Lindsay, like their London predecessors Beatrice and Sidney Webb, failed to institutionalise an applied political science'*, partly because *'the acknowledged expertise did not exist on the basis of which they could overcome official and academic hostility'*, argued Professor Jack Hayward in a study he carried out of how politics grew in Britain as an academic subject. *'Not even the upheaval of a world war, in which some of the few teachers of politics acquired first-hand experience in government was able to destroy the barrier between those whose vocations were the activities of public administration and political service and those whose vocation was the study of politics and administration'*. It was not until as late as 1950 that the British Political Studies Association was established, with Lindsay and Norman Chester, Nuffield's future Warden among its founding fathers.

Moreover, despite the increasing importance of evidence-based social and economic research designed to support public policy-making, there was a painful lack of any empirical appreciation of economics, let alone statistics, in government departments or elsewhere, not least in industry. The generalist male graduate from Oxbridge with a sound knowledge of Greek and Latin literature, ancient history and philosophy seemed to be still far more appreciated than a trained economist or social investigator, let alone a sociologist, in running the country or industry.

At no stage did Lindsay explain in any detail what the new College would be expected to do in the way of specific social research nor how that research was to be organised. It was also unclear who was capable of carrying out such academic work with sufficient rigour in practice. His assertion that the practical men – whether senior civil servants, local government officials or captains of industry and finance – would benefit somehow from coming into personal contact with academics of 'modern' studies in 1930s Britain was based on little more perhaps than an admirable but essentially misplaced idealism. The example of All Souls was an exception with its civilised weekends for the political establishment to fraternise with the Fellows. There was some suggestion that Nuffield College should develop along the lines of All Souls but with a clearer focus on contemporary subjects and applied research.

Lindsay explained that the purpose of research in social studies was to increase social awareness in the community. This did not mean any denial of the importance of university research or research institutions or even of full-time researchers being kept in close touch with the human beings whose relations were the subject of study. But it did mean the development of a *co-operative effort*, however difficult this might turn out to be between the scholar, the trained investigator and the citizen. *'Ideas of this sort were behind the original plan for Nuffield College'*, Lindsay later argued. He suggested the problem considered could be stated as *'What is the scientist to do when his laboratory can be nothing short of the whole community and when his subjects of study are himself and his fellow citizens?'* The basis of the whole Lindsay plan was for the creation of a College where *'the informal cross-fertilisation of ideas may be as important as formal team work.'*

Lindsay knew what he did not want. He was sure that it would be wrong for Oxford to establish a Brookings Institution, devoted exclusively to public policy-making, on the American model. Nor did he suggest the College might turn itself into a Harvard-style Business School. There is no evidence in Lindsay's writings or letters of the time that he looked seriously to the United States or anywhere else overseas in the developed world for intellectual inspiration on how the College might develop. However, the Nuffield concept was influenced to some degree by Lindsay's personal experience of the Christian education colleges in India which he visited during a trip he made to the sub-continent early in 1937. They provided him with an example of how Universities and other further educational institutions might be brought closer to ordinary life. The religious nature of the Indian colleges also appealed to Lindsay who was a practising Christian of the Scottish Presbyterian kind. It is notable that he, as well as Lord Nuffield and Margery Perham, were insistent that the proposed College would contain a Chapel for worship. But what Lindsay clearly wanted to do was accommodate 'modern' studies within the established processes and procedures of one of the oldest Universities in the world that was tenacious in its conservative way of doing things and reluctant to countenance any fundamental reforms that might alter its character. The creation and development of Nuffield College was never going to be easy, as he was the first to recognise. Lindsay as Vice-Chancellor of the University between 1935 and 1938 was well aware of the deep suspicions, envy and even open hostility that existed among many of his academic colleagues about the development of 'modern' studies in Oxford. There were also those who disliked the very idea of a residential College that was exclusively concerned with post-graduate research. In 1937 post-graduate teaching and research was of only limited scope in Oxford and elsewhere in Britain. Those involved in post-first-degree social studies, however widely defined the area was to include anthropology, history, demography, social psychology and law, were few in number. The later Master of University College, John

Redcliffe-Maud, suggested that social research during the decade before the outbreak of the Second World War had been *'amateurish, fumbling and embryonic'*. But if the proposed new College was to develop effectively it would have to recruit high-calibre staff and suitably qualified Students that went far beyond Oxford's limited ranks of potential recruits among its graduates. Lindsay also had to face the reluctance of most Oxford Colleges, who believed the University's ultimate and single-minded purpose was to teach first degree honours courses to young men and women. However, as Vice-Chancellor he went some way to reassure his University colleagues that the new College would not – as his biographer, Drusilla Scott, has written, *'break the traditional forms or alienate the traditionalists'*. His genuine achievement was, however, to persuade the University to change and, *'to come to terms with science and to set the massive Nuffield benefactions on their way with vision'*.

Whatever their doubts or private reservations might have been about the proposed new College, however, the University authorities gave the go-ahead to Lord Nuffield's proposal without delay. In his carefully drafted document to the University's Hebdomadal Council the Founder explained what he had in mind and it seemed to be in line with Lindsay's own visionary thinking. Lord Nuffield later alleged that Lindsay had deceived him about the purpose of the College. But this is not borne out by the evidence. Perhaps the Founder failed to take sufficient interest in what he wanted the College to do and was more concerned to ensure its architecture was in keeping with the older Colleges. But some of Lord Nuffield's thoughts reflected a sensible concern with the general state of British higher and further education at the time. He took the opportunity in his written submission to the Hebdomadal Council, for example, to emphasise the need to encourage a greater intake of university graduates into the world of business: *'I have long deplored the comparative scarcity of university graduates in the highest posts on the administrative and managerial sides of industry, being one of those who believe that there is no branch of knowledge, however 'academic' it may seem, which is not of positive practical value'*, he wrote. Lord Nuffield accepted that most British companies failed to appreciate the qualities that a university education could foster in the young men and women they employed, but he also believed employer attitudes stemmed from the existing cultural gulf between academic studies and practical affairs. *'I should hope the new College would, apart from any indirect effect on the teaching given in the University to the ordinary undergraduate, produce a flow of recruits to industry for whom the gulf to which I have alluded would be bridged'*, he insisted. Lord Nuffield was a man of few words. His initial proposal to found a College devoted to engineering and accountancy, however, was not without its merits. Historically Britain may have been the first manufacturing nation. But the pitiful weakness of the country's technical education was noticeable as early as the time of the 1851 Great Exhibition. The academic status of engineering in particular was extremely low and it remained so for generations, perhaps even up until the present day. In competitor countries, most notably Germany, the cultural hostility towards such a practical but vital subject for economic growth and prosperity was not so apparent. In Oxford in 1937 there were very few undergraduates doing any practical engineering work and most of them tended to graduate with poor degrees. Neither the University nor the country enjoyed a surplus of ambitious and skilful young people who wanted to make their careers in engineering. Perhaps Lord Nuffield's original idea was not as absurd as it was regarded at the time by the University authorities.

There were clearly always a number of diverse, if not conflicting purposes behind the newly conceived College in the autumn of 1937. *The Times* in an approving editorial entitled "Learning and Life" declared somewhat grandly; *'What Bologna did for the public service of the medieval Church, Nuffield College may begin to do for that of modern secular society'*. It then proceeded to sketch out an idealised picture of what the College might become that was very much on the Lindsay lines: *'It will exist to be the meeting-place of men of learning with men of affairs in all departments where their interests may touch, but especially in those spheres of thought and action which make up the domain of the 'social sciences'. Under its roof the diverse specialists engaged in the study of human society – philosophers and economists, historians and anthropologists, jurists and perhaps even pastoral theologians – are to sit down with representatives of the*

AD Lindsay
Leonard Leslie Brooke

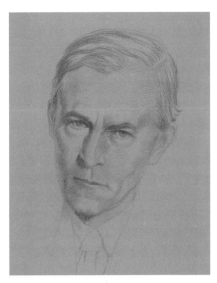

GDH Cole
William Rothenstein

Margery Perham
William Rothenstein

Norman Chester
David Hockney

men actively engaged in the promotion of social welfare – politicians, civil servants, local government officials, and business men. The aim set before this mixed body of scholars and men of the world is, first, that the theories of the one may be constantly tested by practical experience, and the actions of the other founded in a more subtle analysis and a longer view'.

Lindsay accepted that this would involve a *'new method of research'* and that it would take time *'for the theorist and the practical man of affairs'* to secure any fruitful co-operation in working together for a common end. But he thought *'the atmosphere and common life of a college'* would make it more likely and effective. Lindsay believed the time was ripe to advance this development. But he perhaps exaggerated the reality of the current position of the social sciences in higher education at the end of the 1930s. In a BBC broadcast made in March 1939, Lindsay claimed that there had hardly been a University in the previous half-century that had not increased their staff in economics and politics. He claimed substantial funding had been allocated to social studies but the results so far had proved to be disappointing. Lindsay was particularly dismayed by what he saw as the scorn of the practical man for economists who were seen widely as unpractical theorists. However, he recognised that it was not possible to study the social sciences in the same way as the physical sciences. *'For one thing in studying society we are studying something of almost infinite complication where what happens is the result of the interplay of a large number of different factors where experiment is almost impossible and the abstraction usually necessary to obtain scientific accuracy tends to become scientific by becoming remote from reality'.* Lindsay envisaged the proposed College becoming a place *'sufficiently removed from the emotional stresses of politics to make impartial investigation possible'.* He thought that if they were left to themselves, university researchers would invariably *'tend to study only the remoter or more abstract aspects of social questions'.* By bringing them into contact with the men of affairs it would be possible for them to turn the scientific mind onto the questions that people were anxious about and ready to deal with. In this way *'the reproach of the uselessness of social research'* would be removed.

Early Problems before the War

Lindsay's high minded hopes may have inspired some enthusiasts. But during the next two years before the outbreak of the Second World War, the Nuffield College project made only limited progress. The most serious setback to its advance came as a result of the growing antagonism coming from the Founder himself towards the whole idea. Whatever Lord Nuffield's early private misgivings might have been about Lindsay's original conception of the College, they were hardened by what he regarded as the lack of any direct consultation with him on the development of its design or any sense of urgency about starting the building's construction.

In February 1938 a grandiose and totally unrealistic plan was being developed for the College by its governing committee. This would have involved the building of fourteen rooms for the Warden's own lodgings alone with a further eight three-room facilities for Fellows, two or three married quarters, sixteen visitor suites, rooms for sabbatical visitors, ten single rooms for Fellows, forty student two-room sets, six common rooms, a dining hall, chapel, a conference hall, forty research rooms (if possible clustered around the library), one or two seminar rooms, a lecture theatre and finally five rooms for administration. It was also planned that at some future date Barnett House and the Institute of Statistics would join up with Nuffield. *'These requirements were decided without regard to what could be conveniently put on the site'*, Warden Chester later commented. In fact, in one twenty-minute meeting of the College's governing committee twenty-eight rooms were actually added to the original plan.

At least, a greater sense of reality of what was possible, given the size of the College site, appeared to be restored by the late spring of 1938. On 7 May Lindsay wrote to Lord Nuffield to inform him that Austen Harrison, former architect to the public works department in Palestine under the British mandate had been appointed to design the College. His most notable previous constructions were Government House and the Archaeological Museum, both in Jerusalem. Harrison's connections to Britain were somewhat tenuous as he spent most of his time in Cyprus where he lived and at that time he had no experience of building in universities. More seriously, he failed to meet Lord Nuffield at an early stage after his appointment, to discuss with him what his plans would be for the College construction. Harrison was given substantial authority and almost complete freedom to design the College as he so wished. Lindsay made it clear that the University was not going to 'instruct' him on what the College design should look like. He asked only that Harrison would 'advise' the University on his final plans.

The result was predictably disastrous. In June 1939 Harrison unveiled his well-advanced design model for the College in a personal presentation before Lord Nuffield, after it had received the University's unqualified and unanimous approval. It had been generally assumed that Lord Nuffield would simply agree to the design that the committee had accepted from Harrison. But the Founder took one look at the flat-roofed model as it was laid out on the floor in front of him and rejected it out of hand. He complained that the proposed buildings were *'not Oxford'* and *'unEnglish'* and that they failed to respect his known preference for a design which was closer to the kind of Tudor Gothic buildings to be found in Cotswold villages. Moreover, Lord Nuffield added, that Harrison's proposed buildings *'were of an oriental type more suited to Cairo and Baghdad'*. The original design model, which can be found today in the College's Senior Common Room, proposed a long blank wall on the New Road side of the construction, a structure which Lord Nuffield said would make the College resemble a factory rather than a place of scholarship. Lord Nuffield warned that if the buildings went ahead as designed by Harrison he would not allow his name to be associated with the College. Nor was he pleased that Harrison had turned up for the formal presentation wearing sandals and sporting a beard. Veale suspected that the malign influence of Winston Churchill's friend Professor F E Lindemann (later Lord Cherwell) lay behind Lord Nuffield's fierce reaction to Harrison's model because he would have liked Nuffield's money to have been poured into Oxford applied science instead of 'modern' studies. But there is no good reason to doubt that his own feelings were genuinely heart-felt. Later Warden Norman

Chester believed the debacle over the College's original design had a 'disastrous' effect on Lord Nuffield's future relations with the University. Nuffield later complained to Chester that far too much money had been wasted on detailed drawings when only sketch plans were really needed for him to make his decision. It was now nearly two years since he had offered funding for the construction of the proposed College and that was more than enough time, he believed, to have the building well on the way to completion. Instead, it still seemed to be almost as far off as ever from even being started. Lord Nuffield didn't give Oxford University another major benefaction again.

Harrison was forced back to his drawing board in the face of Lord Nuffield's wrath. However, after some protestations he finally agreed to redesign the College to meet the Founder's specific criticisms but considerable time had been wasted as a result. In the summer of 1939 much of the architectural profession deplored the rejection of Harrison's original plans for the College. *'In many ways it was an impressive design, effectively exploiting an awkwardly elongated site and creating a building which would have taken its place among the major architectural monuments of Oxford'*. In the spring of 1940 Lord Nuffield signified his approval of the redesign although adding he wanted a high tower rather than a proposed spired steeple so that the College would be more visible on the Oxford skyline.

The debacle over the original design of the College brought Lord Nuffield's smouldering resentments with the University authorities to boiling point. He was becoming increasingly exasperated by what he saw as the lethargic way in which the College was being developed. Always a rather diffident and prickly man, he had not been kept fully informed in the way that he thought rightly appropriate, and to which he was entitled as the sole benefactor of the proposed College. Lord Nuffield was understandably anxious to see that the College was built and opened during his own lifetime. However, there is no strong evidence to suggest that he was annoyed as early as 1939 with the alleged left-wing Socialist bias of the College and in particular of its

Model of the first, rejected, design for the college

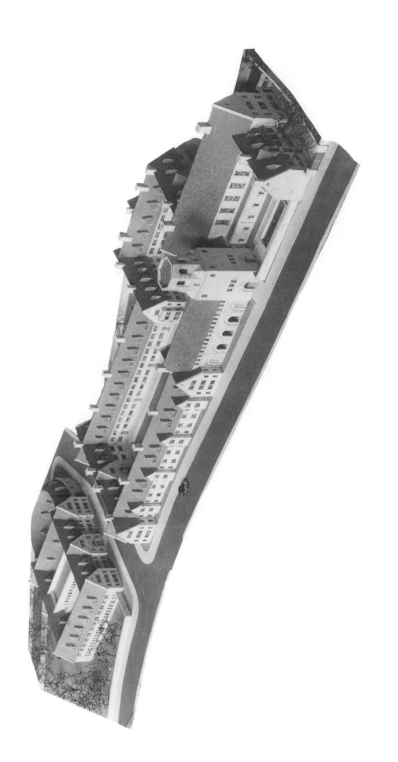

Model of the first approved design

most famous Fellow and Sub-Warden G D H Cole. His friend, the Governor of the Bank of England, Montagu Norman, may have grown used to teasing him about his *'Kremlin down by the station'*. But Lord Nuffield's political hostility really stemmed from later events during the war, concerning Cole and his ill-fated social reconstruction survey. In October 1938 Lord Nuffield even went out of his way to reassure Lindsay, after the Master of Balliol's defeat as an independent parliamentary candidate at the Oxford by-election which was fought over the Munich settlement, that his own personal support for the Chamberlain government's appeasement policy towards Nazi Germany did not mean he bore any personal grudge against Lindsay as a result or that there was *'the slightest risk to our friendship'*.

One of the other initial problems for the College stemmed from the decision to appoint the fifty-four-year-old Harold Butler as the College's first Warden on 20 April 1938 at an annual salary of £1,800 plus £200 expenses. The former Director-General of the International Labour Organisation (ILO) in Geneva hardly seemed like the kind of person to further Lindsay's idealistic but rather vague aspirations for a College that was dedicated to 'modern' studies with either vigour or imagination. An old Etonian with a first-class honours degree in classics from Balliol College and a Fellow of All Souls, his life had been mostly spent in the higher reaches of the civil service at the Ministry of Labour and overseas at the ILO. Veale once unkindly described Butler as an *'idle self-seeker'*. His period as Warden was not deemed to have been a great success. When the Second World War broke out Butler was appointed by the Government as Southern Regional Commissioner for civil defence based in Reading. His absence from Oxford for long periods helped to worsen relations between the College and Lord Nuffield. When Butler returned from the post of Regional Commissioner to the College in January 1942, it was to be for only a short period of time. After just six months back in Oxford, he accepted a post in the British embassy in Washington under Lord Halifax as head of its information services. It did not seem that Butler regarded being Warden of Nuffield in wartime as a sufficiently high enough priority for him. But frustratingly he did not decide to resign as the College Warden until June 1943.

The first academic appointments at Nuffield were made just before the outbreak of war. In June 1939, six Faculty Fellows were announced. They were to continue as Fellows in other Oxford Colleges while taking on their jobs at Nuffield. The most prestigious but also the most controversial was G D H Cole. In some ways he seemed like the ideal figure to transform the College's ambitious aims into practical achievement. An extraordinarily hyperactive polymath who read and wrote across the breadth of the social sciences both in scholarly work and in journalism, Cole was even seen by Lindsay as a possible future Warden for Nuffield. The Oxford historian and journalist Robert Ensor was made a Faculty Fellow attached to the College. He was also a Senior Research Fellow at Corpus Christi. But most of the first Fellows to be appointed to the College were economists. Robert Hall was a College Fellow until 1950 as well as being a Fellow of Trinity College. He was an important figure at the Ministry of Supply during the war and afterwards became economic adviser at the Cabinet Office and later to the Treasury, serving under eight Chancellors of the Exchequer. Sir Roy Harrod was a College Fellow for two stints, from 1938 until 1947 and then again from 1954 to 1958. He was also to be a Nuffield Reader and Fellow in international economics. Peter Oppenheimer, a Nuffield Research Fellow and later a Fellow at Christ Church recalls that Harrod was a *'persistent and somewhat extreme advocate of fiscal and monetary expansion, arguing that an economy must be run under strong demand pressure if it was to realise its full growth potential'*.

An early important area of interest for the College was the Empire and its governance. Sir Reginald Coupland, Beit Professor in colonial history with a Fellowship at All Souls, took a leading part in the origins of the College where he was to become a Fellow from 1939 to 1950. As a young man he had been a member of Lord Milner's famous Round Table, the think-tank of idealistic Imperialists who wanted to modernise the Empire in a liberal way through the encouragement of devolved self-government. A more influential figure in Nuffield during its early years in the area of imperial studies was the redoubtable Margery

Perham. A student of colonial administration, especially in Africa, she was appointed as the College's first Official Fellow in October 1939. Perham was highly effective in establishing a broad network of official contacts in the Colonial Office and across Whitehall. At Nuffield she lost no time in supervising research into imperial government and economics. A close friend of the colonial Governor Lord Lugard, she later wrote an affectionate two-volume biography of his life. Perham herself could hardly be described as an aggressive imperialist. She brought a moral dimension to the governance of the Empire's subject peoples and a commitment to the use of indirect methods of rule based on existing tribal hierarchies.

The first six Visiting Fellows in the College were also appointed before the outbreak of the war. They mainly reflected the world of capital and labour. These were Lord Cadman, chairman of the Anglo-Iranian Oil Company, Sir Walter Citrine, the TUC's general secretary and A P Young from the Rugby engineering works of British Thompson Houston. In addition, Sir George Etherton was elected from Lancashire County Council, along with Geoffrey Vickers a solicitor, and the senior colonial civil servant Lord Hailey.

The Failure of the Social Reconstruction Survey

Inevitably the coming of the Second World War brought an abrupt halt to the beginning of the College's construction. But this did not mean Nuffield was unable to make any useful contribution to the war effort. In fact, the years of total war were to provide the College with the perfect opportunity to test the practicalities of Lindsay's idealistic vision of co-operation between academia and the 'real' world in the solving of common social and economic problems. Warden Harold Butler wrote speedily to the Government's chief economic adviser, Sir Frederick Leith-Ross, on 3 September 1939 – the very day that Britain declared war on Nazi Germany – to suggest that the College should 'get together a group of outstanding persons not eligible for service in Government departments who would undertake special tasks for the government'.

Leith-Ross gave a positive if somewhat guarded response to the Warden's letter and suggested that perhaps foreign refugees and non-British citizens could co-operate with the College in collaboration with the National Institute of Economic and Social Research in London in some research projects that might be of use to the government. However, Leith-Ross added that he could promise no public funding nor any mandate of official approval. Lindsay was not discouraged by this tepid response and appears to have been reassured that at least the Government would tell the College 'what problems we could be most usefully dealing with, that our results would get to the right quarters and our suggestions would be listened to'.

In May 1940 Butler set out a clearer view of the role he envisaged that Nuffield might play during the war. *'I feel the College ought to make some contribution to the problem of social and economic reconstruction, however difficult it might be to organise under present conditions.*

If the College had been in existence when the war broke out, there is no doubt that its constitution and equipment would have given it a special qualification for dealing with the problems of social and economic reconstruction … Its study essentially requires the collaboration of the economist with men possessing practical knowledge of the administrative, financial, industrial and trade union worlds and therefore presents an opportunity for utilising the peculiar combination of experience which the College was designed to bring about'. Butler believed that *'even in its present inchoate condition'* the College *'should not neglect a task for which it is so plainly adapted'*. He went on to suggest that it might be doubted whether any other institution was in a position to undertake such work with equal prospects of success. *'Though some work is being done by other economic bodies in this field most of them and their staffs are actively engaged on problems arising immediately out of the war'*, Butler pointed out. Moreover, none of them had access to the experience of government departments, business and trade union circles as readily as the College had through its system of visiting Fellows.

Butler acknowledged that drawing up reconstruction plans for implementation when a victorious peace arrived was *'a vast and complicated'* matter and that no single body could be expected to be responsible for them. He was convinced that the 'inescapable' problem for the country once the war was won would lie in the prevention of a return to the kind of mass unemployment that had hit Britain after 1920. Butler thought this was a grim prospect that he feared would provoke *'an even greater amount of unrest and greater loss of economic power'* than it had done after the Great War. The Warden envisaged the carrying out of an inquiry by the College into exploring alternative forms of paid employment for workers once the war was over. The aim of the proposed research would be to proceed from *'the known to the unknown'* with a comparison between the economic and social conditions experienced in Britain between 1919 and 1925 and those likely to face the nation at the end of the current conflict. Butler offered himself as the chair of the proposed inquiry and suggested the Oxford Institute of Statistics might be included as a partner in what would be a College-based project. The Warden received warm support for his proposal from Lindsay, Veale and Sir William Goodenough from Barclays Bank, who was chairman of the College trustees. They all believed it would help to calm down and reassure Lord Nuffield who had become *'obviously dissatisfied with the complete stagnation of the College for so long a period'*. Making Nuffield a *'leader of thought'* in wartime, they reasoned, would raise its status and strengthen its legitimacy in the eyes of the public policy world.

But May 1940 – the month of the military retreat from mainland Europe at Dunkirk, followed quickly by the surrender of France to Nazi Germany – hardly seemed like a propitious moment to launch a wide-ranging public inquiry into Britain's prospects in the post-war world, after what then seemed an unlikely victory. Moreover, Butler himself seemed unwilling to abandon his position as the government's Southern Regional Commissioner to take charge of what he was proposing. Goodenough for one was quite bewildered by the Warden's obstinate attitude on the matter. He threatened to resign *'unless the Warden was willing to throw himself with vigour into the work of the College or make way for someone else who could'*. Even if Whitehall were to give the go ahead for the proposed inquiry it clearly required a full-time Chairman as well as a substantial allocation of finance and research staff if it was to prove at all worthwhile.

Lindsay suggested that if the Government itself was not prepared to support an inquiry into reconstruction directed by the College, then perhaps local councils and voluntary agencies might be willing to co-operate in such an exercise. In early January 1941 – at the height of the London Blitz – Cole and Lindsay proposed an inquiry into the social effects of the redistribution of the population that was taking place under existing wartime conditions. A month later this was launched as a national manpower survey under Cole's direction. But from the start, the level of central government support for this proposal remained uncertain. As early as March 1941 Cole was complaining about the unwillingness of the Ministry of Health to co-operate in the examination of local authorities into the future location of industry and population. Ernest Bevin's Ministry of Labour and National Service was even more unco-operative. Local labour exchanges were told not to co-operate with Cole's inquiry. The Warden urged caution on Cole. *'Among other things we have got to be careful to insist on the non-political and scientific character of the survey'*, he warned. *'There is so much mistrust of committees and commissions appointed by the government of the day whatever side is in office that I believe the public would be inclined to place more confidence in an academic inquiry than in a government effort more particularly as Whitehall is in bad odour just now'*.

On 1 April 1941 Arthur Greenwood, the Minister without Portfolio and responsible in the Cabinet for reconstruction plans, announced in the House of Commons that the government had agreed that Nuffield College would carry out an inquiry *'into certain problems of reconstruction and the transition from war to peace conditions'*. *'We expect the results of this inquiry to be most valuable and we hope that the investigators will be given all possible assistance'*, he told MPs. Greenwood seemed to envisage a wide-ranging inquiry that would cover the local and regional organisation of industry, the effect of war conditions on the working of the public social services and those provided by voluntary agencies. It was also to extend to *'the human effects of evacuation, industrial migration and other wartime changes in the conditions of living and their bearing on the problems of social reconstruction'*. But Greenwood was hardly a man of much influence in the Churchill War Cabinet. He had recently been demoted for his incompetence, perhaps as we now know mainly due to his chronic alcoholism. Putting him in charge of reconstruction was a way of removing Greenwood from any direct ministerial responsibility for the war effort without his complete withdrawal from the government.

In May 1941 the Treasury seemed to accept the College's project when it agreed to provide the proposed Nuffield social reconstruction survey with a reasonably-sized grant. Cole wrote to Warden Butler to say his discussions with the Treasury had been *'very satisfactory ... We have been left complete freedom in the use of the grant provided that we meet the normal requirements of vouching and auditing'*, he added. Under Cole's energetic direction the survey quickly began to expand in scope, size and complexity. It soon became unclear to some alarmed observers whether or not Cole was using the College for the furtherance of his own political objectives by means of the survey. As Norman Chester wrote in his unpublished draft history of the College, *'Cole was more a political figure than an eminent scholar. He had been an active publicist in the Labour Movement for twenty years or more. He was viewed with suspicion by Conservative ministers who constituted the majority party in the government and there was not a great deal of affection for him on the Labour side either. The term Nuffield College was largely another name for Cole'*.

Cole's sensitivities were soon upset by the evident determination of the University authorities to ensure that he should not be allowed to take on the position of Acting Warden of the College if Butler agreed to step down temporarily from his position to give full attention to his job as regional commissioner. In a letter to Veale dated 2 June 1941, Cole threatened to resign his College Fellowship if anybody was appointed over his head to that position. He suggested this would be regarded as a *'definite sign of a lack of confidence'* in him were this to happen. *'I am not prepared to give my services to the College unless I can feel that I am being given proper confidence and a status which will enable me to handle difficult government departments and to run a team of university professors which I have got together'*.

By November 1941 the Hebdomadal Council was expressing its growing concern at the way it believed the social reconstruction survey was developing. It passed a resolution that it could not approve of the survey in its current form and insisted it should limit its work to its original, limited aims and not expand into other areas. Cole reacted furiously to such criticism from his University colleagues. *'I cannot remain at my post unless the imputation contained in this resolution is withdrawn'*, he wrote to Veale. But hostility was also becoming apparent to the survey's progress among the Whitehall senior mandarins. The Treasury was already threatening to make cuts in the survey's annual budget allocation while the money taken from the College's own research fund to help in the costs of the fieldwork added to Nuffield's financial difficulties. Cole argued that despite all the problems experienced by the survey it had at least put the *'College definitely on the map'* and done much already to enhance Nuffield's role in the country's reconstruction effort. However, Cole's uncertain position was further weakened by the departure of Warden Butler to the United States in the summer of 1942. It seemed that there was no longer anyone effective or powerful enough in Nuffield to keep a check on his activities. By the autumn of 1942 the government appeared to have grown weary of the whole survey issue. When Butler complained to Cole from Washington that he was greatly disappointed that none of the Nuffield papers arising from the social reconstruction survey had yet been published and that this was harming British relations with the Americans, Cole responded by saying that the reason for this was that the government was insisting that it would ban any publication of material that breached their confidentiality rules. In future, all social reconstruction survey papers were to be treated as if they were Cabinet documents and thereby covered by the Official Secrets Act.

At the same time Lord Nuffield was also growing increasingly angry with Cole's role as the College's recently appointed Sub-Warden and his social reconstruction survey work. In November 1942 Veale wrote to Butler about the Founder's angry feelings: *'He came here boiling with rage about the College saying that he was thinking of publicly disassociating his name from it and making it plain that the University must never expect to get another penny of his money. His rage is now principally directed against our having appointed Cole to look after the social reconstruction survey'.* Veale said he had tried to calm down Lord Nuffield by making a number of propositions; that people who never made mistakes never did anything and that therefore the fact that we had made mistakes did not mean that the original conception of the College was not right and in the highest degree creditable to himself; that as long as it was known that he viewed the College with disfavour he would find plenty of people ready to decry it to him and very few to praise it; and that if his attitude came to be known that he was eminently satisfied that the idea of the College was sound, and that he did not mind a considerable number of mistakes being made by the University as long as the same mistake was not being made twice, he would get a very different account. After an hour and a half of talking like this to him Veale managed to calm down and persuade Lord Nuffield to withdraw his critical comments about the College. But he also demanded that the Founder should give an assurance that in future he would look with favour on the College and the University. Veale added that Lord Nuffield *'looked a bit grim for a moment. Then he put on his hat, flung the door open, shook me warmly by the hand and said 'Well at any rate I will promise to do nothing without consulting you'.*

Veale was increasingly troubled by Lord Nuffield's hostile attitude to his College. *'We failed to keep alive, perhaps even to realise the burning ardour with which he founded it',* he wrote to Butler. *'All his enthusiasm cooled during the months when nothing overt was happening and he heard nothing from us. From the time you came you must share the blame for this with all the rest of us although in fairness to you I must add that if you had found the practice in existence you would undoubtedly have carried it on. If it had been done I believe Cole could have preached the class war from the steps of the College and Lord Nuffield would have borne it'.*

Warden Butler did not agree with Veale's criticisms of the way the College had handled Lord Nuffield. *'We have done everything possible to meet his wishes as regards the building, the appointment of honorary and visiting fellows and in other ways',* he wrote back to the University Registrar. *'If he thinks the College should be conducted on political lines, I do* not see much hope for its future. It has always seemed to me one of the great merits of British universities is that they have always kept clear of the kind of political interference which is common in the USA'. Butler intimated to Veale that he would be 'extremely reluctant' to be involved in the College if Lord Nuffield came to exercise decisive power and influence over its affairs.

But, like Lord Nuffield, Veale was concerned that Cole's expansive direction of the social reconstruction survey was now starting to threaten the College's very purposes. 'I have come to the conclusion that what is wrong with the survey is that it does not carry the fundamental idea of a College. It is a one-sided one-man production such as would be more appropriate to say a department of economics than a College'. In fact, complaints about Cole and his survey were not confined to Lord Nuffield. By the autumn of 1942 they were growing among the University authorities as well as in Whitehall. Veale admitted that Cole was becoming a serious problem. 'My criticism of him is that he pours out endless memoranda containing much that is pure gold but a great deal which I could see for myself on the subjects I understood and which I am told by civil servants who are expected to use his memoranda is just dross. Cole has a fatal gift of being able to dictate perfectly grammatically and with a lucid flow of argument for hours on end. If he had less facility for writing and would produce less stuff all of the best quality which he is capable of producing his position would be unassailable'. Veale was coming to the conclusion that the best plan might be to shut down the survey on its present lines altogether and start it up again with more modest aims.

At its 12 December 1942 meeting the College trustees agreed to send the Vice-Chancellor and their chairman Goodenough to ascertain how the value of the survey work was being regarded by central government through the launch of a 'personal inquiry' in Whitehall. 'This should enable us to dispose of the critics one way or the other. Either their report will be favourable and the critics will be blasted or the report will be unfavourable and the survey will be blasted'. Cole disliked the decision to establish such an inquiry. He complained to Butler on 7 January 1943 that he doubted whether it would be possible to secure 'any categorically favourable answer' from the whole of Whitehall because the survey had meant working with a *'dozen different departments'*. *'I am really in the mood in which I have been so badgered about by one body after another either from the university or from the government that I have ceased to care what happens'*.

In March 1943 Goodenough and his colleagues reported back to the College trustees. It had now become clear that the Treasury would not renew its grant to the survey to cover the 1943-44 financial year and that any future work by the survey team would have to be paid for by way of a fee agreed at departmental level. *'So far as we can ascertain no department with the probable exception of the Board of Trade had any inquiry in prospect which it wished the College to undertake'*, said Goodenough and his colleagues. Whitehall had said that it would do its own reconstruction work in the future and did not need Cole's survey team to help them. Anyway, it was suggested, many of the survey reports that they had been sent were *'too diffuse and sometimes rather superficial. Quality had been unduly sacrificed to quantity'*.

Cole complained to Lindsay in a fury at the government's hostile attitude. *'It is what I expected and it absolutely finishes the hope of continuing co-operation with or without recognition by the government so far as the survey is concerned. If we are to go on we shall have to go on without any government status or recognition and we shall not be able to keep our local organisation in being except in skeleton form'*.

What went wrong with the social reconstruction survey? Cole was always convinced that animosity against him among the Whitehall mandarins was to blame for the failure. He wrote to Lynda Grier, the Principal of Lady Margaret Hall, in May 1943 that while many ministers had shown they were keen on the survey work, both Ernest Bevin as Minister of Labour and National Service, and the Chancellor of the Exchequer Kingsley Wood, had not. No doubt, Bevin like others believed the winning of the war should be the higher priority, not preparing out field work for the peace. His well-known disdain for intellectuals and own personal animosity towards Cole in particular cannot be overlooked in explaining Bevin's opposition to the survey.

'But ministers don't write letters … The civil servants do that and most though not all of them have never really wanted the survey's work and a good many of them have resented it. Throughout it has been a battle to get the civil

service to pay any attention at all. The root of the trouble has been the reconstruction secretariat which was disliked itself and did not want to prejudice its own position by fighting the survey's battles.' Cole suggested a *'civil service junta'* now ran the country except when Churchill himself took a hand or the matter could be *'effectively taken up in the House of Commons'.*

But Cole was also scathing about what he saw as Veale's hostile attitude and that of the Hebdomadal Council towards him and the survey. He believed that he should have been clearly informed about Lord Nuffield's negative attitude towards the survey and given the opportunity to counter it on grounds of academic independence and freedom of research. The core of the problem, Cole insisted, lay in the lack of control that lay in the hands of Nuffield College itself. He did not believe it could be satisfactorily run until its Warden and Fellows were put in charge of its affairs without any permanent outside interference coming from the University authorities. But in 1943-1944 it seemed that the Hebdomadal Council was more in the mood not to reduce but to increase the powers it exercised over the College. Cole thought the University had displayed *'a dislike and distrust of the persons at present in charge of the work of the College – feelings no doubt natural to the reactionary clique that at present dominates the Council'.* Cole wrote to Lindsay on 3 February 1944 that he was no longer prepared to *'retain any connection with the College'* as long as it remained *'subject to a body which has allowed its attitude to be swayed by charges against the work I have been responsible for'.* Cole added that the Hebdomadal Council's behaviour had been *'a disgrace to the academic reputation of the University'* and based on *'violent and unseemly personal prejudice'* against him.

Norman Chester in his draft history of the College believed that Cole had *'probably asked for more status for the survey and more recognition from government departments than would have been normal even in peace-time. Oxford, with an arrogance based on its links to the top of Whitehall rather than on its academic record in the field of economic and social research was not content to undertake research within the limits of wartime conditions'.* In 1974, after reading his account of the social reconstruction survey debacle, Margery Perham recalled to Norman Chester, *'I used to attend meetings of the Nuffield committee at the house in Banbury Road and I always found them most depressing not only because the subject matter was outside my interest or comprehension but I did not realise until I read your history the full degree of Cole's inadequacies. I wonder whether all the vast masses of records produced by the survey have any value now for the historian'.*

There can be no doubt that the bitter controversy over the social reconstruction survey soured the College's relations not only with the University authorities, but with Whitehall senior civil servants, many ministers in the Churchill government and with Lord Nuffield himself. But it also revealed that Lindsay's vision of a College that would provide common ground between the public policy world and academia would be difficult to translate into practical action without a good deal of diplomatic finesse and patience.

The Private Conferences – A Relative Success

However, the parallel experience of the College's so-called private conferences also held during the war proved relatively more successful, at least in so far as they established a personal network of influence between Fellows and important figures in the business community. In 1949 the then Warden Henry Clay admitted to the University Chancellor, Lord Halifax, that the College's private conferences *'had helped to clarify ideas'* on how to make the transition from war to peace by providing the College with *'many valuable contacts with industry and public administration'*. It had also, he maintained, enabled the College to *'build up a body of Fellows who whatever the scope of the future activities of the College were needed to provide a permanent core of people whose primary and undivided loyalty would be to the College'*.

The private conference idea was actually another of Cole's inspirations and it fitted in well with the Lindsay/Lord Nuffield conception of the College's core purposes. It was in July 1941 that Cole first proposed the holding of a series of *'small, very private conferences'* in Oxford under the direct auspices of the College. These would be designed to bring together people from the different mainstream political parties and ideologies as well as business men, trade union leaders and others from the public services. The aim would be to discover whether sufficient common ground could be found between all of them and academics on *'the underlying problems of social reconstruction. The method would be less to discuss what precisely ought to be done in this or that particular field than to consider how the problem of deciding what is to be done can be most fruitfully approached'*, Cole explained.

On the face of it such an idea did not suggest that Cole envisaged the private conferences were going to provide him with the opportunity to draw up a blue print for a socialist transformation of the country. Indeed, in 1941 he did not believe any single political party would be in a position to form a government on their own once the war was won. Like the Nuffield social reconstruction survey, the private conferences were seen by Cole as a means for establishing a kind of national consensus or understanding among the country's decision-makers that would transcend any possible political divisions that might reappear in peacetime conditions. In this, his proposal was in tune with similar activities that were going on elsewhere among the country's political class, intellectuals and business community.

The sixteen Nuffield private conferences which were held during the Second World War attracted an impressive number of public figures in attendance. These included Evan Durbin, the leading Labour revisionist of the time, as well as Conservative social reformers such as Henry Brooke and Quintin Hogg. Young economists, most notably Nicholas Kaldor, Tommy Balogh and Joan Robinson were also frequent participants in the conferences. The calibre of industrialists who participated was equally impressive. Lords Melchett and McGowan came from Imperial Chemicals Industries, Sir Cecil Weir from Glasgow's Chamber of Commerce, as well as Samuel Courtauld, the textile manufacturer, and Sir Raymond Streat, chairman of the Cotton Board. Lord Nuffield did not attend the private conferences himself. He apologised for his absences but said that his business commitments made it difficult for him to participate. He was later to regret he had not been at the private conferences. It was certainly a missed opportunity for Lord Nuffield to exert some positive influence on the development of the College that he had founded. If he had taken a full part in the private conferences he might also have come to a more sympathetic opinion of Cole and his contribution to their proceedings.

What is so striking about the Nuffield private conferences from today's perspective is the high calibre of the men of corporate power in industry and finance who became intimately involved in the affairs of the College during the war and its immediate aftermath as a result. This was not to happen unfortunately on such a scale in later years. Four of the representatives of the forces of capital in particular need more than a brief mention in the history of Nuffield.

Samuel Courtauld built up his family's textile business through a policy of financial prudence and socially-responsible management. He was more than just a successful industrialist. Courtauld played an active part in public life as he pressed for a greater role for the state in the macro-management of the economy. He also took a more sympathetic attitude than most other employers of his generation to the needs and demands of both workers and trade unions. Courtauld was keenly interested in the promotion of the arts and music and he was acquainted personally with the Bloomsbury set. The Courtauld Institute of Art at the University of London in Portman Square is his greatest legacy to the cultural life of the country. But as the College records indicate, Courtauld also took an active role in the affairs of Nuffield, especially during the war and its immediate aftermath.

Sir William Goodenough came from the world of finance. He spent his life at Barclays Bank, following in his father's footsteps and became its chairman in 1943. His entry in the *Oxford Dictionary of National Biography* states; *'He was by nature a conciliator – a trait that made him much in demand on committees of all kinds.'* As chairman of the College trustees Goodenough played a positive role in Nuffield's early life.

Sir Raymond Streat was appointed secretary of Manchester Chamber of Commerce at the age of only twenty-three. He became a redoubtable figure in the College's affairs as a Visiting Fellow. In 1940 Streat was made chairman of the Cotton Board. He had established an important network of contacts as he fought for the interests of the vulnerable Lancashire cotton industry during the Great Depression. But he was also a business lobbyist with a moral conscience and an admiration for William Temple, the radical Archbishop of Canterbury. Streat was an important figure in the governance of Manchester University. As a Visiting Fellow at Nuffield from 1944 and an Honorary Fellow after 1959 he became a loyal admirer of Warden Chester. His published voluminous diaries provide us with some vivid insights into the evolution of the College during its formative years.

Another key figure from the business world who also took a keen interest in the College at that time was Geoffrey Heyworth. He made his business reputation at the soap manufacturers Lever Brothers, at Port Sunlight on Merseyside, and later on when it was transformed into the great conglomerate of Unilever. Heyworth was to be an important influence in the creation of the Administrative Staff College at Henley in 1946 and he became the first chairman of its governors. But his ties with Nuffield were also always to remain strong. As Chairman of the Leverhulme Trust, Heyworth was closely involved in the provision of philanthropic donations to educational research causes. He was also a member of the University Grants Committee. Heyworth was made a Nuffield Visiting Fellow in 1947 and remained on the College's Governing Body for thirteen years until 1961 when he became an Honorary Fellow. Warden Chester recalled Heyworth's value to the College in those early years. *'He was an ideal conversationalist, relaxed, friendly and ready to exchange views on any subject. He was not, however a fluent talker. He did not hold the stage with lengthy expositions of his views on this or that. Often he preferred to listen to what others had to say, an example of his concern with the consumer's opinion. His favourite conversational device was an interrogative statement ending with a kind of questioning grunt. 'It would seem to me', he would say. 'that if that is done this will follow. Eh?'. '*

But for all his apparent reticence, Heyworth was a crucial figure in the development of the social sciences in Britain. Much of his enthusiasm for 'modern' studies stemmed from his Nuffield experiences. As Chelly Halsey remarked in his 1994 David Glass memorial lecture:

> *'Heyworth was thoughtfully practical, came to appreciate the need for systematic and sustained study of an increasingly complex and*

unstable society and was aware that freedom was threatened if people did not have access to collective self-knowledge independently of government'.

It was Lord Heyworth who chaired the committee that led to the launch of the Social Science Research Council in 1965. As Nuffield Fellow Desmond King has written, *'The Heyworth Committee linked social research to the production of knowledge applicable in public policy'*. It was in fact an official recognition of the farsightedness of Lindsay's original vision of linking the practical men to the academics. Heyworth was the kind of man who was able to reconcile academia and the outside world.

Nuffield's first private conference was held in Balliol College in June 1941. Warden Harold Butler assured his audience on the occasion that what they were attending was an 'experiment', consistent with the College's original purposes. There was to be no formal structure to the event. Nor would there be a full report of its proceedings. Lindsay used the opportunity to argue publicly that the private conferences would test the validity of Nuffield's original purpose of bringing the academics and the non-academics together in pursuit of solutions to social and economic problems. He reassured his audience that the College would have nothing to do with *'any contest for power in the political field'*. But Cole was already exasperated by what he regarded as the government's negative attitude towards the private conferences, when it was made clear to the College that senior civil servants had been instructed not to attend any of their proceedings.

In his summing-up of the second private conference that was held on the weekend of 13-14 November 1941 on the subjects of physical planning, post-war building and the future of the cities and countryside, Cole argued that *'unless the government made up its mind on certain major issues, particularly with regard to the responsible authorities for planning, all research would be seriously held up'*. At that time Cole envisaged the private conferences running in parallel with the social reconstruction survey and reinforcing its research activities.

A number of the private conference's deliberations were eventually turned into College pamphlets and published by Oxford University Press. Some of their insights and recommendations are as relevant today as they were in the early 1940s. A study on education and industry that was published early in 1943, for example, called for the creation of technical colleges to be clustered together around what was called a People's University *'with the hope of endowing higher technical education with that cultural quality in which it is now too often deficient'*. The report argued that *'the bias of the education system had been recently against entry to manual occupations but it was of the greatest importance to raise the prestige of high manual skill and to persuade boys, parents and school masters that the skilled crafts offered at least as promising and interesting a prospect and as good an opportunity for advancement as many white-collar jobs'*. The study called for a year of practical workshop training for boys between leaving school and going on into higher education. It also proposed raising the school leaving age from fourteen to fifteen and then eventually to sixteen with compulsory part-time education for everybody between leaving school and the age of eighteen. *'No vested interests'* were to stand in the way of opportunities for education and learning, it declared boldly. The report was signed by forty-five leading people from industry, the trade unions and academic life. Among the signatories were those of the TUC's general secretary Sir Walter Citrine, Samuel Courtauld and Cole himself.

Perhaps the most important of Nuffield's private conference series began over the weekend of 12-13 December 1942. This concerned the issue of full employment in post-war Britain. The discussion was launched by Sir William Beveridge, whose highly influential report on social insurance was actually published that month. He told the conference,

> *'It is not possible to trust to the methods of the last peace – of private enterprise without national planning to bring about the necessary readjustment of our productive effort in the difficult transition period after the war. National planning is essential however the plan is executed.'*

To Beveridge the problem was how to reconcile the *'proved benefits of private enterprise'* with the *'necessity of national planning'*. But Cole admitted in his summing-up of the conference that the discussion had failed to produce any common agreement. The academic economists were unable to convince both the industrialists and trade union leaders of the positive interventionist role into industry that the state needed to play in resolving the problems of high unemployment and inflation.

As a result, that particular private conference ended inconclusively but it was only adjourned to be resumed for a further session over the weekend of 27-28 February 1943, in the hope of reaching a common agreement. Cole took a more optimistic view than others in believing that it would be possible to ensure there was a return to full employment once the war was over. Economists were convinced that they could reach an agreement that would ensure the familiar peaks and troughs of the economic cycle would grow less volatile if state action was taken. But to ensure success it would necessary to establish a voluntary understanding between employers and trade unions on the reforms of the economic structure that would be required in order to guarantee full employment without inflation. Cole went on to suggest a new spirit would be required in industry through the whole-hearted recognition by employers of trade unions, the continuation of joint production committees, a purge of monopolistic influences, a national minimum wage, control of prices and wages and a public code of conduct on how companies and trade unions should behave to one another. Cole attacked *'monopoly profits'* that would seek to *'exact from consumers and workers an excessive margin from the necessary costs of production'*. But none of these proposals met with the approval of the employers at the conference. Just as significantly Sir Walter Citrine from the TUC and a Nuffield Visiting Fellow expressed his opposition to any state intervention to control wages which he believed workers would not accept. He argued any such move would deny them the freedom of voluntary collective bargaining between employers and trade unions. The deeply-rooted post-war obstacles to a national programme of economic and industrial modernization, agreed between capital and labour, were therefore already apparent in the proceedings of the Nuffield private conferences.

The resulting report from the private conference on full employment was published in May 1943. It proposed a plan for industry that would seek to *'attain full employment'* and recommended the creation of a national development board and a Minister for National Development as well as the creation of permanent Works Councils for employees at factory level in peacetime to replace the current joint production committees. The Communist party newspaper, the *Daily Worker*, praised the document and headlined its story; 'Big Business Men Advocate More State Control for Full Employment'. Although *The Times* argued in an editorial that the report was *'constructive'*, it worried about what it saw as *'a rather alarming advocacy in extensions of state control which would place power in the hands of those least competent to wield it – the civil service'*. The 1943 Nuffield report proved, however, to be an inspiration to Beveridge when he wrote his important book that was published in the following year – *Full Employment in a Free Society.*

The College's private conferences certainly revealed a new, more positive attitude by some of the country's larger employers on what the role of the state should be in the future macro-management of the economy. But their apparent conversion to the economics of demand management and the concept of a 'mixed' market economy with a strategic role for the public corporation, did not extend to any willingness on their part to endorse moves that would either weaken or challenge their power and authority in the workplace or enterprise over their employees. Cole was delighted to hear *'economic heresies of the past'* were now *'proclaimed as economic truisms'*. But the Nuffield conferences failed to bridge the genuine gap in basic attitudes that existed between the academic economists and the business-men towards the state's direct intervention in the affairs of industry. The employers who attended the private conferences held their ground on the need for corporate self-government in the private sector rather than any direct government control of their activities. Cole may have been infuriated by the attitude of the employers but on the other hand he was also anxious to retain their support if at all possible. The 1943 private conference document on industry and the economy was therefore inevitably a necessary compromise, primarily designed to placate the employers and to ensure they went along with what were watered-down proposals. Its conclusions owed much to Cole's tactful diplomacy and the employers present were ready to acknowledge this. But as an article by Daniel Ritschel of the University of Maryland on Nuffield's private conferences published in *Twentieth Century History* in 1995 argued, *'the widespread cynicism about business practices voiced in the discussions on industrial organization was, in the end, deliberately subordinated to the desire to secure the adherence of businessmen to an agreed statement on full employment. The uneasy consciences of the cynics were salved by an appeal to the beneficial effects of Keynesian economics. The compromise reached at Nuffield thus employed the promise of full employment to harmonize the participants' fundamentally divergent views on industrial reconstruction'.*

A further important Nuffield private conference was also held during the weekend of 9-10 December 1944 to discuss Beveridge's new book under the heading of industrial organisation in relation to a full employment policy. Sir Raymond Streat wrote in his diary that it was to be *'one of the best'* of the conferences that was held during the war. What many of the Nuffield private conferences indicated was that while there was a genuine willingness to find common ground between capital and labour, crucial differences of interest remained considerable. Voluntary self-restraint by workers in full employment conditions would be required to avoid the need for state controls and regulation. But as Warden Clay admitted; *'The discussions had not got very far with plans for securing the wholehearted co-operation of all sections of the community'.* In truth, there was a failure to find much strong common understanding between the employers, academics and others who participated in the Nuffield private conferences. *'The price of business endorsement of the progressive agenda of full employment, social reform and a large public sector in a mixed economy was the abandonment of the progressive vision of a state-supervised strategy of industrial modernization and a grant of practically unfettered monopoly powers to the private sector'*, noted Ritschel. Hope instead was placed in the belief that the social solidarity that had been achieved under wartime conditions could somehow be carried over into the peace through a subtle combination of goodwill and flexibility.

Nuffield College's activities in wartime – through both the ill-fated social reconstruction survey and the relatively more successful private conferences – were hardly subversive. They reflected much of the progressive conventional wisdom of the time. Moreover, Cole himself was keen to deny that he was intent on using the College as an academic institution which would somehow further the creation and development of a full-blooded socialist programme of reconstruction. *'Nuffield College as a research institution has itself no collective opinions'*, he explained. *'Its responsibility is limited to approving the scope of the work undertaken and to satisfying itself that adequate steps have been taken to maintain a high standard in performance'*. Despite occasional outbursts of ideological enthusiasm, Cole by the early 1940s had grown very much into a man of the 'middle way' although like so many others at that time he envisaged an increasing expansion in the role of the central state in social and economic affairs. Always an energetic enthusiast, however, Cole could take a critical view of the employers in general, including those at the private conferences. This was also apparent in his attitude to the use of the state. At the March 1942 private conference on prospects and policy for Britain's post-war export trade in relation to the location and distribution of industry, for example, Cole told his audience that it would be a mistake to think that in peacetime the country could maintain the industrial structure and attitudes that it had done before the war:

> *'We will have to make much more substantial changes in the structure of Britain than many people have yet contemplated … This is not only a matter of knowledge but very much a matter of the temper and attitude of those responsible for framing economic policy'*.

Cole did not believe it could be simply left to private financiers to decide the allocation of capital investment. The state must ration and direct.

The employers involved in Nuffield College activities may not have agreed with such opinions but many were nevertheless impressed by Cole's abilities as the summariser at most of the private conferences, even if many of them opposed suggestions from him that in the post-war years there would have to be a radical industrial restructuring with more power, control and responsibility handed over to employees and the trade unions. Samuel Courtauld spoke warmly of the *'almost magical skill'* with which Cole produced a sentence embodying *'a common*

58

measure of agreement in a few lucid words in the middle of a cross fire of suggestions'. 'Cole's firmness and expression of any personal views have been equally remarkable', he added.

It is interesting to note that for all his public reputation as a radical socialist or even syndicalist, Cole during the war years proposed an entirely new purpose for Nuffield College that would have been beneficial in the long term to employer interests. He wanted to turn the College into a management training centre. *'We have now got a good set of contacts with the business world and I do not want to let them slip'*, he wrote to Warden Butler in October 1942. Cole said he intended to prepare a proposal for the introduction of management training at Nuffield. Butler did not dismiss the suggestion out of hand. *'The idea of a staff College for business men and civil servants is certainly interesting'*, he replied. However, Butler thought it would be better if Nuffield were to provide *'education for managers but not in management as a technical subject'*. Cole was convinced that his idea would not breach the existing College Statutes. He thought his proposal could begin with the selection of more Visiting Fellows from the business community to Nuffield and the holding of summer schools in the College for the training of management. But Butler, on reflection, rejected the management school proposal and it died in 1944.

Nuffield College's involvement in the Second World War was not confined to the Home Front. In his draft history of the College, Chester wrote that Nuffield had achieved one notable success in its efforts to establish some common ground between academia and the world of public policy-making. One piece of successful research was carried out by College Fellow Sir Reginald Coupland on the Indian constitutional question. But the main wartime achievement in Nuffield research on imperial matters was most evident in the work done on colonial administration under the energetic direction of Margery Perham. This did not receive the kind of hostile publicity secured by Cole for the social reconstruction survey, and nor did it provoke bitter conflict between the College and Whitehall. Perham's activities were respected at the Colonial Office. A series of well-received Nuffield books were published on colonial legislatures and the dependency of colonial economies, especially in Africa, as a result of the wartime survey activity. They were designed to provide signposts for the post-war world in Britain's colonial policy although there was no suggestion that the country's colonies should be given their political freedom. It was all the more unfortunate that Perham began to feel she was under-appreciated by the College. In February 1945 she wrote a plaintive letter to the Warden seeking a pay rise. Perham pointed out that the *'young men'* just starting their careers and employed by the College were earning almost as much as she did despite her long years of experience and list of publications. She told the Warden that in the post-war world the College could take on important work and responsibility for research on the future of the colonies in which *'British social and political ideas'* could be applied to their problems. *'I do feel rather discouraged if when we appoint new permanent fellows to the College who are eminent in their subjects they are automatically put into a higher category than myself on the grounds that they were men, they had to be attracted here and they had wives and families'*.

Warden Chester in his draft history, while appreciative of Perham's contribution to the College, admitted that many Nuffield colleagues regarded her as being outside the mainstream of their interests. But he recognised that *'the ideas underlying the foundation of the College were ideally suited for her'*. Perham's world was not only made up of African chiefs and peoples, colonial governors such as Lord Lugard and district officers but also government ministers, newspaper editors and senior civil servants closer to home. Perham's wartime work was to ensure a continuing tradition of research interest in the College for both colonial and imperial affairs that still continues at Nuffield to this day. Many prominent historians of the Commonwealth, most notably David Fieldhouse and Freddie Madden, were influential Fellows of the College during the 1960s and 1970s. Today John Darwin keeps that tradition strong. But Megan Vaughan's election to a University professorship in Cambridge led to the abolition of a second post in the College for imperial history.

Perham's influence was also apparent in her enthusiastic assistance to a number of students who were later to become substantial figures in post-colonial Africa, such as Kofi Busia. Although he was never at the College but at Ruskin, Tom Mboya, the charismatic Kenyan politician, was also strongly influenced by Perham.

The experience of both the social reconstruction survey and the private conferences during the war highlighted some of the strengths but also the weaknesses of Lindsay's original vision for the College. He himself assessed the position of Nuffield again in 1946 in a rather sombre mood. *'It has not been possible to build and the College exists in the most meagre accommodation. It has not been possible to make the influence of the Visiting Fellows nearly as intimate and continuous as was hoped.'* Lindsay acknowledged that it was often difficult to maintain a constant contact in *'the more theoretical fields like economics and political theory'* between the scholars and the *'world of action'*. *'It made a considerable difference to T H Green in the nineteenth century that he had played a part in politics and all the difference later on to Graham Wallas.'* Lindsay recognised that in the past *'economic theory suffered from its abstractness from real life and from sheer ignorance as to how business men actually behave'*. He acknowledged that the College was only at the beginnings of working out just what the best method could be for achieving fruitful co-operation between *'the University's staff and other citizens'*.

In 1949 Henry Clay, the Warden, told Lord Halifax, the University Chancellor that while Cole's social reconstruction survey had moved *'outside its original bounds'* in doing so it had brought the College *'into effective contact with a large number of industrialists, trade union officials, members and officials of central and local authorities, educational experts and social workers'*. The private conferences as a result had been particularly useful after the social reconstruction survey was wound up in providing the College with *'many valuable'* links to industry and public administration. Clay was convinced that it had also *'enabled the College to build up a body of Fellows who whatever the scope of its future activities were needed to provide a permanent core of persons whose primary and undivided loyalty would be to the College'*.

Unfortunately the Nuffield private conferences were not to be continued in any systematic way after the war ended. They did not become a prominent institutional arrangement for the Labour government in its construction of the 'new Jerusalem'. A few were, however, held after 1945. One took place in July 1947 which dealt with the country's increasing difficulties in external economic relations. Two years later another focused on the problems of managing large industrial organisations as key sectors of industry were brought into state ownership.

One senior figure in the Labour government found time to become involved in the College through attendance at such gatherings. This was Herbert Morrison, in effect the deputy Prime Minister as Leader of the House of Commons and Lord President of the Council in the Labour governments of 1945-1950. He agreed to become a Visiting Fellow at the College while still a member of the Attlee Cabinet. Morrison made the opening address to the College private conference held in September 1949 on the public accountability of the newly nationalised industries. Out of government after Labour's general election defeat in October 1951, he worked in the College, helped by Norman Chester and Kenneth Wheare in writing his authoritative book, *Government and Parliament*. Morrison admitted to Sir Raymond Streat that his book could never have been completed without the help and inspiration that the College provided him. Morrison was a constitutional traditionalist in matters of parliamentary affairs. But his volume was well received when it was published in 1954. Morrison enjoyed coming to the College during the 1950s and in his final years he was made an Honorary Fellow. Some former Students like George Jones of the London School of Economics – one of Morrison's co-biographers with Bernard Donoughue – still remember him as a friendly conversationalist over the College's breakfast table.

Nuffield's penultimate private conference was held in July 1955. This was to coincide with the tenth anniversary of Victory in Europe day. The list of participants was impressive. They included Hugh Gaitskell who was elected Labour leader four months later and Harold Wilson. Reginald Maudling and Edward Boyle – junior ministers in Sir Anthony Eden's recently re-elected Conservative government – also attended. There were senior civil servants present like Sir Frank Lee, permanent secretary at the Board of Trade, and Sir Leslie Rowan, second secretary at the Treasury. The economists included Frank Paish, Robert Hall and Thomas Balogh. The conference mood was optimistic about the future outlook for the British economy. A paper from Austin Robinson on the balance of payments was dismissed by many participants for being unduly gloomy. Most of those in attendance expected steadily rising productivity, improved living standards and no return to the mass unemployment of the 1930s. Warden Chester pointed out that if a similar conference had been held ten years after the Great War in 1928 it would have been obsessed by mass unemployment and industrial unrest. The contrast with what was widely perceived to be a benign economic situation in 1955 was palpable. The College's final private conference was held at Worcester College in October 1955. This was to discuss the recently published report from a Royal Commission on the future of east Africa.

Recruiting the Best

There were some important changes in the leadership of the College during the war and its immediate aftermath. Henry Clay was elected as Nuffield's second Warden, succeeding Harold Butler in January 1944. His earlier career had included work in adult education before the Great War, a stint at the Ministry of Labour and a Fellowship at New College. Clay was a political economist and in 1922 was appointed to the Stanley Jevons Chair in that subject at Manchester University where he stayed for eight years. He then took up a position at the Bank of England under Montagu Norman where he helped in the financial reorganisation of the depressed industries. By the end of the 1930s Clay was more or less a Keynesian. He took an active part in the founding of the National Institute of Economic and Social Research in 1938. Under the direction of Lord Stamp, Clay also played an important role in the development of economic forecasting and statistics in the period immediately before the outbreak of the war. He was the author of a number of books on political economy, including *The Problem of Industrial Relations* and *The Post War Unemployment Problem*.

In 1944 Clay's task as Warden was not regarded as an easy one to take on. *'We could not see how to carry out the purposes we had been given. Our constitution was as complex and restrictive as a Chinese box'*, recalled Margery Perham. *'There were material problems not only about the ultimate building of the College but problems about immediate accommodation, residential housing for Fellows, equipment, and finance and all of them had to be resolved without the help of all those precedents, large and small and those habits of association which, in older societies, lubricate the machinery of administration until it seems to run almost automatically'.*

Perham admitted that Clay *'did not fill the academic vacuum with large and masterful plans of his own'.* But perhaps more importantly he was successful in linking up the College more closely to the University after the traumas of the war years caused mainly by Cole and his social reconstruction survey, by Lord Nuffield's growing hostility to the College, and by Warden Butler's apparent lack of vigorous leadership because of his absences. Perham believed that Clay was a *'good ambassador'* for the College because of the way he disarmed *'prejudice by his wisdom, simplicity and astringent humour'.* She used the opportunity of the April 1949 luncheon for Clay on his retirement to spell out the problems of 'modern' studies in reconciling academic autonomy and scholarship with the demands of the state and the outside world. 'We of this generation of Fellows know quite well that we have still to find out how the College should set about the task that the Founder has set us', she explained. Perham called for the 'understanding and help' of the University as Nuffield went about its developments. But she also pointed perceptively to the particular difficulties that were facing academics in their researches of the modern world.

> *'Our study of contemporary affairs has its special perplexities above all when the wheel, the last revolutions of which we are watching not only will not stop for a moment but seems to be turning ever faster as its pattern, becomes more crowded, intense and more ominous'.*

Perham drew attention to the research problems involved.

> *'We have to draw evidence in due proportion from life and from the book – too often the blue book with its peculiar and most arid form of language. We have to remain in alert contact with action and men of*

action without allowing them to tempt us too far from rationalisation into participation. We have to attain, if we can, the proper degree of the judicial in the treating of subjects in which our prejudices, our political commitments, our national and even our personal interests are engaged. In our kind of work we must often go into a partnership in our research with Whitehall and the problem of preserving the old freedoms of the University within the new regimentation of the endangered state is perhaps especially hard for us'.

Perham warned her audience in 1949 that they must recognise that Nuffield had only just begun to build itself into a College and it would not achieve its *'full design for many generations'.*

During the 1940s under Butler and Clay the College began to appoint Fellows who were to pursue their research interests in 'modern' studies. Although few were recruited during the war years, it was soon evident that the Fellowship appointments were going to prove difficult and even contentious in what was regarded as a rather sparse field of talent outside the ranks of the academic economists.

There was one particular incident that did not reflect well on official attitudes inside Nuffield towards internationally-renowned scholars in the social sciences. In November 1944 Lindsay proposed that Karl Mannheim, the famous sociologist from Frankfurt University who as a Jewish refugee had fled from Hitler's Germany, should be made a full-time Research Fellow in the College. He was at the time a special lecturer at the London School of Economics and Political Science and recently naturalised as a British citizen. But Mannheim's academic position in Britain remained insecure and he was seriously contemplating a move to a university post in the United States. Lindsay believed that he was the greatest of living sociologists and thought he would make an invaluable bridge in the College between the economists, political scientists and anthropologists. Lindsay's recommendation to appoint Mannheim was considered by a College sub-committee. It decided to offer him a University Readership rather than a full College Fellowship. But Nuffield's executive committee then proceeded to turn down the recommendation of Mannheim for the post in February 1945. There was clear evidence of an anti-German bias in the decision. It was Visiting Fellow Sir Raymond Streat who took the decisive step in what was to be done to Mannheim's application. He wrote fully about the whole wretched affair in his private diary: *'There was quite a debate about two Europeans – Mannheim and P Good as they were, I said we were engaged in collecting keystones for a new Anglo Saxon edifice in the heart and centre of Anglo Saxon culture and therefore we ought not to have any foreigner, however brilliant, until the spirit of Nuffield was firmly created out of Anglo Saxon elements. Later foreigners could be added but not at the stage of foundation stones. Curiously enough both Clay and Lindsay had not seriously considered these aspects before suggesting two foreign names. They admitted at once that my arguments must prevail'.*

The appointment of Fellows began to consume increasing attention during the final months of the war. As Streat again noted in his diary: *'At the meeting of the Warden and Fellows there was a long talk – with deep currents under the suave words – about how Official* [full time] *Fellows were to be appointed. Here lies the kernel of the real academic future of Nuffield because the type of men will determine the type of work'.*

In the immediate post-war years the College was inevitably focused on the prosaic task of appointing suitable Fellows and planning for the eventual arrival of Research Students. The most pressing problem was the need to press ahead with the building of the College in what were difficult circumstances. There were obviously more important national priorities for construction work in the aftermath of the war's destruction of houses and industrial plant. Tight restrictions on the granting of planning permission and the provision of building materials were real headaches for the College authorities.

Britain in the 1940s was hardly a country that enjoyed a surplus of suitably qualified academics in the social sciences available either at Oxford or any other university outside the London School of Economics and Political Science. In 1947 Norman Chester, then a Fellow of the College for only a year and a half, admitted to Warden Clay that of economists who might be persuaded to leave their existing jobs, only Cairncross and Bretherton (both in the Treasury) were possible appointees. *'There is nobody I would recommend strongly on the government and public administration side'*, he added. *'As you know the field here is pretty thin, being composed of one or two well established people such as William Robson'*.

But Warden Clay was successful in attracting one rising star among Britain's political theorists to a Nuffield Fellowship – Michael Oakeshott, from Gonville and Caius College in Cambridge. His efforts to recruit a man who was already a leading Conservative academic thinker does not suggest that Clay was particularly concerned about the impact such an appointment would have on the rest of the College. He wrote to Oakeshott on 4 December 1947 that while Nuffield might not be able to offer any accommodation unlike *'an old foundation'*, it could provide a reasonable income to someone who wanted less interruption in his attempts to think and write than most university teachers enjoyed. Clay added that he and other Nuffield Fellows were still acutely conscious of *'the need for more work in the field'* in which Oakeshott was working. *'Our little group has become more firmly established; the University respects us and has reason to be grateful for the additions to its teaching strength which the economist Sir John Hicks, Chester and the younger Fellows have voluntarily made'*. Nothing came of Clay's initial approach to Oakeshott. But a year later on 4 September 1948 the Warden wrote again to Oakeshott about coming to Nuffield as an Official Fellow. *'I have the impression that things are moving very much in your direction'*, he revealed. *'Painful experience has convinced a few people that political ideas are important and experiments in the organisation of society to accord with ideas other than theirs must predispose people to listen to yours.'* Oakeshott was duly appointed. But he stayed for only a short time before moving on to a Chair at the LSE where he spent the rest of his academic life. He was succeeded at Nuffield by another distinguished political theorist, John Plamenatz.

One of the negative consequences of Oakeshott's association with Nuffield was the creation of a personal conflict with the eminent political theorist, Isaiah Berlin, which lasted for most of his life. In a letter he wrote to Shirley Letwin, Oakeshott's daughter and his putative biographer, in November 1991 Berlin recalled that he had first met her father at lunch in Nuffield. *'It was a friendly lunch'*, he recalled. *'But when I said that he should write something on Hegel, he seemed to resent it and then things went badly.'* Berlin said that Oakeshott also made a *'bitchy introduction'* when he gave a series of lectures at the LSE soon afterwards. *'He told people that he had beaten me for the Chair at the LSE for which I never applied. So things did not go well'.* It was another twenty years before the two men met again. *'He was very affectionate in a tipsy sort of way'*, recalled Berlin of that occasion. *'He asked me who is the greatest French thinker of the twentieth century and brushed aside my suggestion. The answer was Paul Valery which upset me but not gravely.'* The mutual acrimony between the two men that had first begun over the lunch table at Nuffield was intellectually destructive to both of them. Berlin told Letwin bluntly that he had *'never read a word'* of Oakeshott. *'I know that his way of thinking is in some ways similar to mine but –.'* However, she sent him a copy of her father's book, *Rationalism in Politics.* Berlin said he would read it. *'I shall now set sail on this boundless sea without seeking harbour. In your brilliant essay on Hume and Oakeshott I think you exaggerated his quality. I adore Hume. Perhaps I will now come to adore Oakeshott.'*

Oakeshott's appointment to Nuffield in 1948 was, however, something of a coup for the College. But not all attempts to attract substantial scholars were as successful. Strenuous efforts were made by Warden Clay, for example, to attract the distinguished social anthropologist Barbara Wootton to the College from Bedford College at the University of London but they failed.

The relative paucity of established academic talent available in the social sciences in Britain at that time was reflected in the findings of the Clapham Committee in 1946. It discovered there were only thirty-five professors in the whole country in the field, which was defined widely to include economics, anthropology, demography, statistics, sociology and political science. *'It is doubtful whether even at the present day the great practical value of knowledge in these various fields is generally appreciated'*, admitted the committee's report. Sir Michael Clapham, who was an eminent economic historian, and his colleagues revealed the under-developed nature of the social sciences and their possible use to the world of public policy making. It might have been expected that the demands and pressures of war would have changed official attitudes.

68

This does not seem to have been the case. The post-war situation might have cried out for a diligent focus on the encouragement of the academic social sciences. It was not at least for another ten years that decisive action was taken. As the Clapham report explained; *'It is a platitude that modern industrial communities rest on the knowledge of the subject matter of the natural sciences. It should also be a platitude that their smooth running and balance rest upon the knowledge of the subject matter of the social sciences. Social services cannot be properly planned without the knowledge of social needs and social responses. Economic policy cannot be properly reviewed without the knowledge of economic quantities and economic institutions'.* The report asserted it was not sensible for the state to rely on hunch or traditional wisdom in the development of social policies. But it also admitted that *'even where the importance of this kind of knowledge is recognised it is doubtful whether there is a parallel recognition of the importance of providing the resources which make it possible'.* In social studies Britain's universities in 1946 were in fact, as Clapham's committee acknowledged *'under-staffed and under-endowed'* in the areas where Nuffield College sought to carve out a role for itself.

However, this was not true of economics. The College recruited a number of first-rate economists at the end of the war. David Champernowne was Nuffield's first economics Official Fellow when elected in 1945. He came straight from working at Bletchley Park where he had been part of the vital cipher-cracking team which had helped to win the war by breaking the German military codes. Champernowne became Professor of Statistics in 1948 and he remained at Nuffield as a Professorial Fellow until 1959 when he moved to Trinity College, Cambridge. *'He was a remarkably clever man who did various things, all imaginatively and lucidly and always in his own novel and distinctive style',* Christopher Bliss has written. *'Perhaps his reputation suffered because he spread himself so thinly, covering both economic theory and statistics'.*

Herbert Frankel was also elected to the College in 1945 as Professor of Colonial Economics and he remained at Nuffield until 1971. Bliss has claimed that Frankel was *'a deep thinker, but too often out of tune with his contemporaries to enjoy the appreciation that he arguably deserved'.* He was a monetarist before the term was widely used and as Bliss argues *'Frankel saw the use of a currency as the product of a relationship between government and public based on trust. Such thinking seemed eccentric and oddly right wing at the time'.*

The other distinguished economics Fellow was John Hicks, an Official Fellow from 1946 until 1952, he was then elected to the Drummond Professorship of Political Economy at All Souls. Bliss argues that *'despite his greatness it is hard to detect any Hicks imprint on Nuffield or even on Oxford in general. His creative period was over by the end of the war and he subsequently worked and wrote in such a peculiar and individual style that had anyone wished to become his disciple it is far from clear how they would have done that'.* However, the prominence of three distinguished economists suggested the still unbuilt College was already attracting some of the most brilliant in the country.

Much public satisfaction was expressed at Nuffield's progress when the College's foundation stone was laid at a ceremony held on 21 April 1949. The Chancellor, Lord Halifax, claimed on that occasion that while there had been more than a ten-year delay in starting work on the building of the College the delay *'had not been without its advantages'.* Not only had it shown the *'foresight by which the new venture was inspired by those who had doubted the expediency of giving such direct encouragement to graduate studies it would acknowledge their claims and the need of institutions to serve them'.* Lord Halifax added that the war experience had *'compelled experiment'* and as a result *'a small but not undistinguished'* society of scholars had emerged with a life of its own before even a brick had been laid. To the Chancellor, the Nuffield College project represented an attempt *'to meet new needs in ways that accorded with the traditions of Oxford'. 'It meets the needs of graduate students pressing on the University and it does so by providing them with a collegiate society adapted to their special circumstances.'* Lord Halifax took a characteristically high-minded view of the College's ultimate purpose;

> *'There is no incompatibility between the recognition or the practical exigencies of everyday life and the search for underlying principles. It should be the aim of the philosopher and statesman to establish common ground between ultimate aims and immediate expediencies so that their respective champions may march together. In times like*

these a group of students who devote part of their working life to this high object will do society no small service'.

It was unfortunate that Lord Halifax's sensible words were heard by few of those who were attending the foundation stone ceremony either because the amplifier did not work or somebody had failed to switch it on. Sir Raymond Streat wrote in his diary that after the Chancellor's oration, *'There was a fanfare from the band, Lord Halifax moved forward to draw the chain through the pulleys – the Warden gave Lord Halifax a silver trowel which he declined to soil with mortar, preferring to borrow a utility instrument from a mason – several trowels smoothed mortar round, experts improving on his Lordship's inexpertness, coins of the 1949 minting were dropped in a cavity below the stone and finally with some fussing and adjustment the stone was laid, tapped on each corner by the Chancellor and then proclaimed by him with whimsical solemnity to be 'well and truly laid'. Prayers were said by the College Chaplain, the National Anthem was played and the ceremony was complete'.*

At the celebratory luncheon held in the dining hall of nearby Christ Church after the ceremony, the newly-appointed Vice-Chancellor seemed to cast some doubt on the familiar refrain about the gap between academia and the world of practical men. *'There is a certain amount of cant about what is sometimes said about the purity, the aloofness and remoteness of academic pursuits'*, he insisted. *'I do not think that really squares with our practice in fact. If this College devotes itself more consciously and explicitly to the study of the contemporary scene it is really I think only putting more clearly what all of us have been doing all the time.'* Warden Clay at the lunch argued that the new College would offer the opportunity to clarify *'the current confusion about means and ends that arose from the multiplication of committees, boards, departments, unions and organisations'* which so often *'provided no more than an excuse for shirking the hard task of thinking out what as a society we really want and may reasonably hope to have'.*

The foundation stone ceremony and the luncheon were both attended by Lord Nuffield despite his known complaints about the College's progress. But he must have found the event rather a strain, especially when Clay used the occasion to praise his predecessor Butler as well as Lindsay and Cole. *'This is gall and wormwood to Nuffield; all three are* bêtes noires *so far as he is concerned'*, Registrar Veale whispered to Streat over the lunch table. *'I take Veale's remarks with reservations but the evidence is fairly general that Lord Nuffield can be obstinate and wayward'*, Streat noted in his diary. *'Anyhow today he was mild and unimpressive – just remarking that he hoped the College would at least improve the appearance of his native city'*.

On reflection, Streat ruminated in the privacy of his diary on what he saw as the purposes of Nuffield College to which he was now a Visiting Fellow. His strongly expressed views would have been unlikely to have pleased Clay and Lindsay if they had known what they were at the time: *'Nuffield College is concerned with the so-called social sciences. At this time our economic system is in a state of chaos and under a socialist government our conventional social structure is being reshaped with violent haste. Academic discussion and academic enquiry into the theories of social science seems a little like fiddling while Rome burns. Yet perhaps nothing is more important than that some competent minds should be situated outside the maelstrom of current affairs, trying to discern and define fundamental principles. I feel that the basic idea behind Nuffield – or at any rate one of the chief ideas behind it – namely to make a bridge between academic thought and the practical world has much potential value in it. The difficulty is to get the busy men in the outer world to spend enough time in Oxford for the intellectual communion to mean much for either party. The effort* vis à vis *these outsiders needs to be more intensive than Clay with his modesty has made it'*. However, Streat concluded his gloomy thoughts in a more positive frame of mind. *'It is not every day that there is laid a foundation stone of a new College in one of the oldest of the still existing seats of human learning. On such a day a participant would be dull indeed if he were not prompted to some ruminations on history and life and what have you. Thank you Lord Nuffield. I would buy one of your cars if the Labour government allowed you to sell them on the home market'*.

Streat's diary entry on the College's foundation stone ceremony also revealed just how difficult it was going to be for Nuffield to assert the importance of 'modern' studies in a sceptical Oxford University at the end of the 1940s. As he wrote, reflecting on the events of the day,

'The community of cap and gown, living in their ancient and honourable colleges conveys a sense of combined antiquity and continuity which is in strange contrast with our ever changing and rather battered world. The present office holders seem just the same as their innumerable predecessors – concerned with study, exchanging visits, talking of the qualities of absent members of their circle, discussing college affairs, recollecting the peculiarities of this or that professor or college head, remembering a good dinner or a good joke. It is all of a high level of intelligence and culture but all remote in a peculiar way from the kind of harsh realities which dominate life and talk in Manchester, for example'.

Warden Clay sought to relate Nuffield's progress to the original Lindsay vision. In a signed article that he wrote for the *Manchester Guardian* on 21 April 1949, he emphasised that the College would be a place where scholars and policy-makers could work together, free from the stress and pressures of the modern world. As Clay explained; *'The ordinary university teacher is overwhelmed with teaching and routine administration as never before. The civil servant who has to organise and administer this new world is so pressed with day to day duties that he has little time to think. The politician and his unofficial advisers who are designing the new world are equally pressed with current business and usually lack both the systematic equipment of the scholar and the contact with administrative actualities of the civil servant. To this need Nuffield College must make a small contribution of great if transitory importance; while in the long run it has a distinctive part to play in the organisation of graduate teaching and research in its own field and that of the University'.*

The first Stated Meeting of the Warden and Fellows on the College's New Road site was held in November 1950. Streat emphasised the uphill progress they had experienced in getting the go-ahead for the building of Nuffield in the restrictive atmosphere of the times. It had been decided to use the Warden's completed lodgings for the gathering although it was surrounded by a *'wilderness of mud and builder's litter'.* *'Everything in the Lodging is in unstained oak and Cotswold stone',* Streat noted. *'The ceilings are low and the windows small, both perhaps to fit in with the external conception which is a blend of Oxford College and a Cotswold small country house. But it is a creation full of an intimate charm and with a character and an air all of its own. It will be different, I think from anything in Oxford at present. It can hardly be said to express the spirit of the twentieth century for it is not modern except in its interior fitments but it shows the skill of the twentieth-century designers in creating a special place in a special setting.'*

The arrival of the first Students in 1945 was a further step in the making of the College. Most of Nuffield was operating from 17 Banbury Road and 70 Woodstock Road. The arrival at the New Road site was to take place in phased stages as different parts of the College buildings were completed. Those early Students recall a friendly, informal atmosphere after 1950 but they also reflect on their difficulties in trying to study on what was still not much more than a building site. As Glenn Willson, later Vice-Chancellor of London University, remembers: *'The only negative aspect was the irregular and unnerving 'thump' of pile driving during the laying down of the foundations of the new building. How long that went on I cannot remember, but it made concentration particularly hard!'* But to Willson, the College before its completion in 1958 was *'primarily a place to drink tea or coffee, and to have lunch; it took a little time to appreciate that one had the opportunity to take part in the development of a fully cohesive and self-conscious community'.* What he recalls in particular is the four-way division of the College at that time between the economists, Africanists, trade unionists and the politics people.

'The division rarely, if ever, generated friction, and it was by no means complete – one was aware of the interest in the impact of each on the others when discussions of broad themes were under way. But for most of the time we all seemed to go along very separate roads, speaking in very different tongues. I must say that there was little apparent concern for the development of any integrated discussion of The Social Sciences. Sociology was viewed with grave suspicion. Everybody was magnificently obsessed with their own projects, and that produced an atmosphere full of energy and stimulation which must have contributed towards a consciousness of common ground – but it did not seep out as discussion of over-arching theory'.

Willson also reflects that Nuffield College was regarded in the early 1950s by much of the rest of the University with *'a mixture of curiosity, scepticism and even some hostility … There was a sense of being on sufferance.*

The whole notion of serious academic study of contemporary events and problems appealed to many as more appropriately the job of good journalists, and the analysis of how things were actually done in the real world was not specially welcomed in a setting devoted to reflection in depth at a decent distance in time. On occasion, criticism was quite hurtful. At the same time, there was also a good deal of respect shown for the College as a fledgling elite body. And we were the first College to house both men and women, which on the whole was well received – deservedly so, for relations within the College seemed to me admirably civilised from the beginning'. It was, in fact, only after 1959 that women Students were actually allowed to live as well as study in the College.

Jenifer Hart was made a Research Fellow at the College by Norman Chester when he pointed out to her that she was too old to become a Student after her years employed at the Home Office during the war. In 1951 she was made the first Gwilym Gibbon Fellow in order to carry out research on the relationship between central and local government in the administration of policing during the nineteenth century. *'The atmosphere of the College at first was informal as our premises were various north Oxford houses'*, Jenifer Hart recalled in her memoirs. *'Snooty arts people have tended to denigrate Nuffield as a philistine institution but for me the social and intellectual life it provided whilst I was a Fellow and indeed thereafter for many years was of enormous benefit.'* Hart was particularly impressed by what she regarded as the high degree of gender equality in the College at a time when the rest of the University remained hostile or indifferent to the very idea of women graduates. *'Such was the chauvinistic, demeaning attitude of the University that it was not even possible for dons in men's colleges to ask a woman to a meal in Hall or into the Senior Common Room. These restrictions on social life were not significantly relaxed until the 1980s but at Nuffield sex equality reigned from the start. When I was one of the few women in the College I did not feel any difficulty. I was treated as a person not as an oddity and was neither sidelined nor harassed'.*

In her memoirs Hart wrote fondly of her love affair with Michael Oakeshott during his brief time as a Nuffield Official Fellow. *'On meeting him I was at once fascinated by his darting, twinkling eyes and his boyish Bohemianism and I found there was much about his way of life that appealed to me; he was unconventional, rejected ostentation and was an incurable romantic'.* But Oakeshott was also a Conservative political philosopher. *'The experience of men and affairs was a far better guide to action than trying to apply an ideology,'* he told Hart and that before considering whether to make various changes *'one should study tradition, history, customs'.* She did not share his hostility to the post-war Labour government and was not converted to Conservatism but they remained close friends and they wrote affectionate letters to each other for at least a few years after he departed to the LSE (these are contained in the Oakeshott papers in the LSE Library). Hart gave a flavour of life at Nuffield at that time in her correspondence with him. In one undated letter she wrote to Oakeshott. *'MP* [Margery Perham] *gave a very revealing seminar on Lord Lugard but I unfortunately missed it. She passed round his boring diaries and pictures of him apparently and is reported to have been very emotional about everything. I don't go there very much now and I normally only seem to hit off dreary overseas students when I do. They all have the views of old men and think I am trying to épater them. If I say I like modern architecture i.e., Corbusier and not Nuffield'.*

After years of debate and discussion, the lengthy process of building the College was virtually completed by 6 June 1958 when the Duke of Edinburgh flew by helicopter from Windsor Castle to hand over to Nuffield its Royal Charter. At the luncheon that followed, which was the first meal served in the completed College Hall, the Duke gave his own characteristically blunt views about the social sciences and what he regarded as Nuffield's purpose to the assembled gathering, which included both Lord Nuffield and Lord Halifax. He conveyed the already firmly held view that the College was resolutely pragmatic and based firmly on empirical facts in its academic pursuits.

'The objective study of the way people manage their economic problems, their social lives and their self-government cannot fail to have a real and lasting value on human society. Not in the old fashioned and misguided belief that it can produce a sort of Utopia but in the belief that a better understanding of these problems may prevent some of the worst mistakes'.

The Duke told his distinguished audience that they were *'really still like children'* when it came to *'intangible social studies'*. But he warned them to avoid *'the frustrations of a petty-fogging bureaucracy or the slow poison of industrial relations'*.

> *'If Nuffield can dig out and lay bare the true facts of human tensions and frictions it will certainly not produce any noticeable increase in human happiness but it will at least help to lubricate the rather creaking machinery of man-made institutions.'*

A Student, Tony Quainton (later an American ambassador to Nepal and to Nicaragua), recalls the day vividly. *'Susan* [his wife to be] *became faint during the ceremonies in the Hall and retired to my office. We were then, some half-hour later, surprised by the Duke* [of Edinburgh] *and Norman Chester touring the College. I think the Duke thought he had caught two Nuffield students* in flagrante. *Happily nothing of the sort was the case.'*

The 'Golden Age' of Norman Chester

I do not think the University has really ever tried to understand what we are trying to do. I think it has always assumed we are something rather odd.

Norman Chester to the Franks Commission 18 February 1965.

We are ... different in purpose from other Colleges.

Norman Chester in his Valedictory Address to the College's Governing Body on 10 June 1978.

Norman Chester's Vision

Nuffield will always be associated with the name of Norman Chester. He was the College's Warden for nearly a quarter of a century – from 1 August 1954 to 31 July 1978. More than any other man, including even A D Lindsay, he was to shape the ethos and traditions of the College as he sought to reconcile its various original purposes with Oxford University, the world of the public policy makers and the academic social sciences. *'Chester attended to every detail of its building and administration. Even today there is hardly any aspect of the College that does not bear his imprint'*, David Butler said at Chester's memorial service in 1986. A bluff Mancunian, with ruddy cheeks and a bushy but always well-groomed moustache, Chester needed to display remarkable patience, tact and self-restraint in the difficult years he spent as a College Fellow before his eventual election as Warden in 1954. Made a Fellow in November 1945, he had been a possible candidate for the Wardenship after Clay's retirement in 1949. Chester discovered that some Fellows had wanted to put his name forward as their sole candidate when Sir Edward Bridges, head of the Civil Service and former secretary to the War Cabinet, turned down the Wardenship. But he admitted at that time 'he was deeply conscious' of 'his shortcomings'. Chester then went on to become an indispensable administrative support for the rather ineffectual Alexander Loveday during his five years as Warden. But despite this he was not regarded as the obvious successor when the position again became vacant.

In October 1953 the College Fellows unanimously agreed to offer the Wardenship to the Oxford historian of political ideas, Isaiah Berlin, then a Fellow of New College. *'I hope this will not be a very great disappointment to you'*, Margery Perham (who as Senior Fellow was presiding over the Wardenship election) wrote to Chester. But she was anxious to reassure him that the Fellows continued to hold *'a great affection'* for him and appreciated all that he had done for the College under Loveday. *'If Berlin accepts we shall have a brilliant Warden but we shall need more than ever all the great service you have given to the College'*, she added. However, after some agonising that went through what he described as several *'slow and painful stages'* Berlin turned down the offer but with regret. It was probably a wise decision. As Berlin admitted himself, *'Being as I am and my interests being what they are I should always feel that I am insufficiently close to or representative of what I regard as the true and proper central purpose of Nuffield'*. Noel Annan wrote in *Our Age* that Berlin also took a rather dim view of sociology, arguing it had never produced *'a single thinker of any significance – no, not even Max Weber'*. Berlin's abilities as a College administrator, however, became much better known ten years later when he turned out to be a very successful founding President of Wolfson College.

The College Fellows went on to offer the Wardenship to Kenneth Wheare, holder of the Gladstone Chair of Government and Public Administration in the University and a Fellow of All Souls. He lost no time in refusing the post, explaining privately that he did not want to stand in Chester's way. Perham told Chester that she admired him for the way he had behaved during a *'time of great strain and anxiety. I have been full of admiration for the way you have come through it'*. Other prominent figures were also considered by the College's selection committee to be Warden. These were thought to include Sir Oliver Franks and Oxford economists Robert Hall, Sir John Hicks, Sir Roy Harrod and James Meade. Finally it was unanimously agreed to offer the position to Chester on 6 February 1954. *'I am afraid I was not very articulate on Saturday morning'*, he wrote to Perham *'when with such characteristic kindness you personally conveyed to me the invitation of the executive committee. It was a moment for which I had greatly hoped. When it came, however, I was overwhelmed by the unanimity of the invitation'.*

In fact, Chester was the ideal man to become Warden at that time. Born in 1907 (in Chorlton-cum-Hardy), the son of a cotton textile worker, he left school at the age of fourteen to work in the treasurer's department at Manchester town hall. A self-educated didact, the twenty-three-year-old Chester won an external BA degree at Manchester University, where he also gained an MA in 1933. After three years of research, Chester was made a lecturer in public administration at Manchester University in 1936 and later in that decade he held a Rockefeller Fellowship for a year based in New York. At the outbreak of the Second World War he was recruited into the economics section of the War Cabinet secretariat where he later worked closely with Herbert Morrison and Sir John Anderson. His most memorable wartime posting was as secretary to the Committee on Social Insurance and Allied Services, which was chaired by Sir William Beveridge in 1941-1942.

Chester may have been seen as an Oxford outsider by some in the University; an intruder from the industrial north. But he was always keen to uphold Nuffield as a College dedicated to the pursuit of high academic standards. Chester was anxious to secure the approval of the University authorities for the legitimacy of the College as a recognised institution of rigorous research in the best Oxford traditions. In later life Chester was disappointed that he was not made chairman of the Royal Commission on Local Government. The position went to another Oxford luminary – Sir John Redcliffe-Maud, Master of University College. But Labour Prime Minister Harold Wilson did later appoint Chester to be Chairman of a Committee on Association Football and then of the Football Grounds Improvement Trust. Chester was never offered a peerage but he was knighted in 1974.

As an academic, Chester wrote a number of dry but reliable volumes on public administration. He was one of the founders of the British Political Studies Association when it was established in 1950. Three years later Chester wrote the rules for the newly-formed International Political Science Association, of which he was president from 1961 to 1964. *'This is an example of a major contribution institutionally and intellectually that the College made at the beginning'*, says Laurence Whitehead, now Nuffield's Senior Fellow. Chester was also highly influential in the early development of the European Consortium of Political Research. His outlook was never to be insular. In addition, Chester was the capable editor of the academic journal *Public Administration* for more than twenty years. *'He was a productive, meticulous and wide-ranging scholar'*, says David Butler, who was a close academic colleague and for eight years the College's first Dean and Senior Tutor. *'He wrote with clarity and precision rather than with stylistic sparkle, his works making a notable and authoritative contribution to the study of parliament and administration'*.

'Chester remained very much a northerner, always keeping something of his Mancunian accent', added Butler. *'His occasionally blunt rejection of the conventional Oxford style upset some people and earned him a reputation for being abrasive. But behind the apparently rough exterior there was a man who showed great kindness to colleagues and to students'*.

A H (Chelly) Halsey, a College Fellow in sociology, contrasted what he saw as *'the two caricatures of English notables'* in an essay on Nuffield and Chester. In the first *'things happen to one. One is sent to Eton, finds one's way into politics or the civil service, is called to imperial service and is in short portrayed as having led a life of effortless superiority leading to inevitable and impersonal success. The second follows the more difficult path from what used to be called provincial obscurity by the scholarship ladder to professional achievement and public recognition. He typically emerges as a striving individual out of the solidarity of the 'working-class movement'. His education is owed to standing three-deep in obscure bookshops in northern industrial towns and he struggles to the top. If these be the only two categories then Norman Chester belongs to the second'*.

Halsey believes that Chester's conception of the College grew strongly out of his strong Mancunian background. *'His intellectual outlook was faithfully fashioned by the civic traditions of Manchester – a University which was conspicuously successful in the earlier part of the twentieth century in striking a balance between cosmopolitan scholarship and realistic practical concern with its immediate industrial environment through the application of natural and social science to its problems.'* In Halsey's opinion, Chester intended and quickly effected a fundamental modification of the older collegiate traditions of Oxford at Nuffield which, while making it distinctively modern, always did so within the framework of what was acceptable to a University that remained at best unsure of the rigour and legitimacy of the social sciences.

The letters of congratulation Chester received from prominent people in the outside world must have reassured him and boosted his self confidence as he moved into the Wardenship. *'I am sure it will be a good thing for the College'*, the former Labour Cabinet minister Herbert Morrison wrote warmly to his old friend. *'Your admirable work not only for the College but for the University generally and your other activities in the public interest not only deserve to be recognised but give you excellent qualifications for the responsible duties of the Warden.'*

One of the most important tasks that Chester set for himself during his earliest years as Warden was to reconcile the estranged Lord Nuffield to the existence and well-being of the College. He paid close attention to the Founder's sensitivities and he displayed considerable diplomatic tact in what was the painful process of healing the rift that had opened up between Lord Nuffield and the College since the summer of 1939. Sir Raymond Streat, as a Visiting Fellow, recognised the difficulties posed by the Founder to the College he had endowed after attending the first Governing Body meeting under Chester in November 1954, when for once Lord Nuffield was present: *'He is definitely uninspiring. I have always thought so. One finds it difficult to understand at first why he made so much money and secondly why he gave it away so imaginatively. However, he is without doubt one of the most creative benefactors in history and as such must surely be honoured. He gave a drab little speech of five sentences with an absurd story about some municipal orator who spoke too long. It had no point in it. They tell me that at times he has been very displeased with what was done or might be done at Nuffield College but apparently Chester has got on his right side and relations are now very happy'*. Chester's deliberate charm offensive proved to be highly successful. He even established a Founder's Day celebration in College in 1959 that was to commemorate Lord Nuffield's birthday each year. By the time of his death in 1963, Lord Nuffield had grown reconciled to the outcome of his benefaction and was more positive in his attitude to the College. While previous Wardens had tended to neglect or avoid making any consistent effort to establish better relations with the College's Founder, Chester went out of his way to keep Lord Nuffield fully informed of what the College was doing. Indeed, it would be no exaggeration to suggest that he and Lord Nuffield became close personal friends by the end of his life. *'The Warden treats him like a rich, elderly uncle'*, reflected Streat in his diary on 13 June 1957. Halsey saw their relationship as benefiting from a *'particularly happy coincidence of personality'*. The important practical implication of this was that the College became the residual beneficiary in Lord Nuffield's will (although he had given so much away that, after death duties, this only amounted to £500,000). As Halsey has written, *'Thus a rapprochement of the 1950s by contributing to the College finances in the 1960s helped to meet the threat to a small but independent centre of support for the social sciences in the financially harsher climate of the 1970s'*. With no children as heirs to his enormous personal fortune, Lord Nuffield left his spacious country house, Nuffield Place at Nettlebed near Henley, to the College. It was to be used over the years by Nuffield Students in search of greater solitude to write their dissertations or as a haven of peace and leisure for anybody connected with the College who want somewhere to relax. Summer parties were also held there for Nuffield Fellows, Students and staff where Warden Chester showed what a demon he could be on the croquet lawn.

The reconciliation with the College could be seen in 1957 when he made sure that the College buildings were completed successfully. A word from him led the Nuffield Foundation to provide a further £200,000 to complete the building of the final two staircases in the lower quadrangle. *'When I first became Warden we had not got enough money to finish the buildings and we used to talk about the choice of having Fellows and no buildings or buildings and no Fellows'*, Chester told Lord Franks's committee of inquiry into Oxford University in 1965. *'This is still in evidence in the balance of our Fellowships. At one time we could not look far enough ahead in connection with our money to have all our Fellows on long term Fellowships; even Official Fellows were sometimes on three-year Fellowships which were renewable. Even now, a high proportion of our expenditure is on things which could be cut down if the question of income failed to meet the essential expenses.'*

It is interesting to note that Chester suffered an early verbal assault from the College architect, Austen Harrison. This concerned the proposed height of the Tower, which Lord Nuffield insisted should become a prominent feature of the Oxford skyline. Harrison wrote angrily to the Warden on 17 December 1954, *'I am told you show the model of the College to all and sundry to elicit opinions on, among other matters, the height of the Tower. This action is consistent with your contention that one man's opinion is as good as another. But has it occurred to you that this habit betrays and advertises a regrettable lack of faith in your architects which is not circulated to increase their chance of achieving a satisfactory building? Did I think your contention true I would, in our own interests as much as in yours, advise you to invite every don in Oxford today to say how high the Tower should be; to average the answers and to instruct your architects accordingly. In this way you would be relieved of a responsibility which you now unnecessarily undertake and which you find onerous. Once after a meeting at Nuffield which your architects had found more than ordinarily arid and cyclic a Fellow, observing signs of our distress, courteously volunteered the information that the methods of discussion by which you reach decisions were characteristic of the University and ultimately derived from those of Socrates.'*

By the mid-1960s Chester had come to regret what he saw as the perhaps inevitable decline of the College as a closely-knit academic community where Fellows and Students could mingle together amicably for their mutual benefit. Between 1954 and 1965 Nuffield doubled the size of its annual Student intake to around thirty. The Warden observed that the time had now passed when senior Fellows tried to keep in touch with everything that went on in the College. He reflected that while a few of them might manfully attempt to maintain personal contacts with all the Students, others seemed to feel that the best they could do was to know those Students who were in their own or closely-related subject areas. This development may have been unavoidable as the College grew but it gave Chester cause for concern. He still remained convinced that the ideal of the College was as a small community of the academic and non-academic engaged in common endeavours. A commitment to a unitary or integrated Nuffield was still the primary objective. *'I would judge it a bad thing if the College broke up into groups – economists, historians etc.'*, Chester confessed to the Franks inquiry.

The Warden had mixed feelings about the role of the Official, Professorial and Faculty Fellows and the College officers as Nuffield increased in its numbers. He believed the amount of time that they devoted to pure research would suffer as other responsibilities became increasingly important and onerous to them. Chester had in mind government assignments, television performances, teaching and graduate supervision, as well as examining students and carrying out faculty administration. Although he accepted that some Fellows kept away from such activities, he also acknowledged that neither the University nor the College could function effectively if every Fellow confined themselves to their own research and writing.

The presentation of written and oral evidence to Lord Franks' inquiry into Oxford University provided Chester with the opportunity to set out his considered views on the future of the College after the experience of just over ten years as Warden. He was clearly determined to establish limits on Nuffield's capacity to expand in order to meet the growing demands of the social sciences in the University and beyond. Nearly thirty years after Lindsay's original vision, the social sciences were beginning to become more important in Britain's higher education system. The newly formed universities of the early 1960s, known as the 'plate glass' universities, were setting the pace. Most of them were establishing large social science departments. The creation of the publicly-funded Social Science Research Council in 1963 – much influenced by Nuffield's Visiting Fellow Sir Geoffrey Heyworth who became its first Chairman – testified to official government interest in the subject area as well. But Chester was not keen on the idea that in response the College should expand the size of its intake of Fellows and Students in order to meet the undoubtedly rising demand for places at Nuffield coming from within Oxford University's own walls or from other places. Nor did he believe that the College must shoulder all the burdens and responsibilities of the social studies faculty. Nuffield was not to be regarded as an institution of teaching. Its Students were there to carry out post-first-degree research. The annual intake needed to be restricted to no more than thirty Students in order to uphold the highest academic standards. Chester was always an unrepentant meritocrat and he resisted pressures to open up the College to a much larger number of Students. As he argued before the Franks Commission, *'There is little justification for the post graduate Student who is less than first class.'* Chester wanted to keep Nuffield deliberately small and exclusive. He described the College as *'a small body of Fellows and Students living and working together in a large but nevertheless contained and homogeneous field of study and research'*.

Chester was well aware of the problems that were facing post-graduates as they carried out their research projects for doctorates. This is why he saw the College as an important academic institution that could help to support them at a time when such assistance was not widespread or available elsewhere. *'Even the most buoyant and extrovert of students experience periods of depression – the material they need is not readily available or is less suitable than they thought; they are having problems of presentation; the writing is proceeding slowly and the likely date of completion is receding. Unlike the undergraduate who may be one of two hundred or more working for the same papers in the same way with the same examination deadline the graduate may be quite isolated, working on a subject only his supervisor and possibly two or three others are interested in and very dependent on himself for the date of submission'*. This is why, in Chester's opinion, a College like Nuffield was so beneficial for the well being of post-graduate students. *'The essence of the College system and the justification for its continuation is that undergraduates are likely to develop better, more academically and generally in small communities of teachers devoted to their interests than in large university departments. These independent, democratically-governed societies are also likely to provide a better and more attractive academic environment than hierarchically conscious departments.'*

Chester set out what he regarded to be the important factors that underpinned the success of a graduate College in front of the Franks Committee. He stressed the need to provide graduate students with *'the fullest possible'* facilities on the 'hotel' and 'club' side as on the academic. *'One will not get the best out of them unless one regards them almost as junior fellows.'* The Warden said that at Nuffield Students ate together with the Fellows at lunch and dinner *'free of charge at a common table'*. Nuffield also *'ideally'* provided all of them with residential suites made up of their own study-living rooms in the College as well as adjoining bedrooms. Nuffield, he said, was also willing to provide incidental expenses to Students and Fellows such as the cost of travel to use a library in Edinburgh, for example, or within reason to collect material in other countries.

Such generous financial provision also meant it was necessary to keep the number of Students in the College relatively low. Chester added that Nuffield never took anybody merely because they could pay their way for their education or rooms. It was an admirable feature of the College that the majority of its British Research Students came from state school backgrounds and not the private sector. *'The College is more flexible than an ordinary university department'*, Chester also explained to the Franks inquiry. *'Our appointments are not tied to any particular teaching need or specialisation. We have the widest possible discretion in the types of Fellowship or other appointments. We can therefore shift our interests fairly quickly depending on current needs and the availability of suitable people. Our mixture of Oxford residential College and specialist department plus the close links we have established with the world of practical affairs should give us some advantages.'*

But Chester was well aware of what he saw as the *'temptations or dangers'* that threatened a residential Oxford college whose focus was exclusively concentrated on research into contemporary subjects. *'Very few academics are single-minded about research'*, he lamented. *'They are strongly lured into teaching and lecturing, visiting professorships abroad and faculty business as well as examining.'* In addition, for some Fellows at Nuffield there were *'the tempting claims of public affairs, sometimes involving a lengthy leave of absence'*. The Warden recognised such *'distractions'* might guarantee a full and interesting life for the Fellows but he believed they also threatened the research and writing that should be their primary concerns.

However in 1965, as in the past, no clear consensus could be established on what the purposes of the College should be. Chester acknowledged that Nuffield had *'probably favoured learning for its own sake'* too much and this was not good for what he regarded as its primary objective, which he believed should be to research and try to resolve contemporary economic and social problems. Highly-qualified people were what the College was seeking rather than the encouragement of particular subjects of perceived current importance. But Chester also appeared to sympathise with the view that the College should become in effect more of a training centre for the education of future academics and this is what happened. In the 1960s a remarkable number of Nuffield Students were to take up teaching posts in the expanding universities where social studies departments were developed as well as in Oxford colleges who were each recruiting their own economists and political scientists. The first four members of the newly formed politics department at the University of Kent in 1965 came from Nuffield, for example. A substantial number of Students also secured Oxford Fellowships in other colleges during the 1960s as many of them felt the need to recruit qualified academics in 'modern' studies to teach their undergraduates. But Chester continued to wonder whether it made much sense to increase the actual number of Students elected to the College if it meant the provision of extra places *'for Americans, nineteenth-century historians or philosophers'*, none of whom he believed were in short supply. He told the Franks inquiry that he saw no point in diluting the quality of students who came to the College or adding more of them to the number because they provided better hotel facilities or in the mistaken belief that they were providing them with a training that was not available elsewhere in Oxford. *'In so far as the College has spare resources I would sooner see them used to elect extra Official Fellows with new fields to develop (for example, the American economist Martin Feldstein) or more Research Fellows in interesting subjects'*, Chester explained.

Nuffield College in the Public World

Under Chester, Nuffield College was certainly able to acquire a more substantial role for itself in public affairs. Many government ministers, trade union leaders, senior civil servants and a few business men, found that Nuffield was very much the place to be during the 1950s and 1960s. Some came often as Visiting Fellows. A regular flow of them descended on the College to give seminars, attend High Table dinners and Governing Body meetings and to discuss particular issues with Fellows and Students. Their presence enabled those who resided in the College often to establish productive relations with them in the outside world. This could lead to important public appointments or at least access to government departments. In the 'golden age' the non-academics in Nuffield's life looked like a cross-section of Britain's metropolitan elite. They included Conservatives like Reginald Maudling, Sir Edward Heath and Willie Whitelaw as well as senior Labour figures such as Sir Jim Callaghan and Shirley Williams. More recently Jack Straw, Patricia Hewitt, Tessa Jowell, David Miliband, David Willetts and Vince Cable have been Visiting Fellows. Union leaders were also frequently to be seen in the College in those days where they had become a force to be reckoned with. These included Jack Cooper, Bill Carron, Len Murray and Jack Jones. *Guardian* editors were also predominant among the Visiting Fellows – notably A P Wadsworth and Alastair Hetherington. Today's *Guardian* editor Alan Rusbridger is a Visiting Fellow along with the newspaper's star columnist Polly Toynbee. But other senior journalists were also to come to Nuffield as Visiting Fellows in the 'golden' age, most notably Sir William Rees Mogg from *The Times*, as well as Donald McLachlan from the *Sunday Telegraph*, Samuel Brittan of the *Financial Times*, and Geoffrey Goodman from the *Daily Mirror*. Nor were leading industrialists entirely missing from the ranks of the Visiting Fellows. Prominent among them were Sir Maurice Laing and the more controversial Jim Slater. Sir Campbell Adamson came from the Confederation of British Industry (CBI). Richard Lambert, the current director general of the CBI, former editor of the *Financial Times* and one-time member of the Bank of England's Monetary Policy Committee is a current Visiting Fellow. But there were far fewer figures from the business community in the 'golden age' and in later years than there had been during the College's early years. Senior civil servants were also prominent among the more illustrious of the Visiting Fellows. These included Sir William Armstrong, who was involved with the College from 1964 to 1972, as well as Sir Ian Bancroft the redoubtable Dame Evelyn Sharp and Sir Richard Wilson. Numbered among other Visiting Fellows are the penal reformer, Vivien Stern, Sir Ian Blair, the Metropolitan Police Commissioner, and the director of Liberty, Shami Chakrabarti.

But it is not clear just what most of those Visiting Fellows really contributed to College life in a tangible way. Some gave seminars on a Saturday morning after the Stated Meeting each term. The list of names and topics suggests they must have provided stimulating and informative sessions to those who attended. Sir Edward Heath gave a session in November 1962 on the government's negotiations that he was conducting to take Britain into the European Economic Community. The machinery of economic planning in government was the topic for a discussion, led by Sir William Armstrong and Sir Donald MacDougall in March 1967. The Labour government's prices and incomes policies were discussed by Shirley Williams and Jack Jones on a number of occasions during the 1970s. But there are no verbatim records of what took place at those events and nothing appeared to happen in the way of a follow-up. The sessions were held under the self-imposed restrictions of the so-called Chatham House rules. This ensured there was a high degree of confidentiality that was probably unnecessary for most of those occasions. The lack of any systematic use of the Visiting Fellows by the College is apparent during the Chester years. It can be seen as something of a lost opportunity. Certainly many Students believed they could have benefited from holding more public and structured meetings between them and individual Visiting Fellows. It was often only by pure chance that the Students could strike up conversations with them over the breakfast table. Apparently many Visiting Fellows felt the same way about the lack of contact with the Students. As one of them put it, he did not regard his position at the

College as merely an addition to his *Who's Who* entry. It was to be their constant complaint that they had no real idea of what they were supposed to be doing as Visiting Fellows and they regretted the lack of personal contact with the Students. Jose Harris, a Research Fellow from 1969 to 1972, vividly recalls a long session of informal talk with Shirley Williams that went into the early morning. But as most of the Visiting Fellows were leading busy public lives, they needed a much clearer definition of what their functions in Nuffield should be. In the standard letter inviting them to become a Visiting Fellow, the College did spell out what it expected but only in very general terms. The obligations required of them seemed rather minimalist. They were asked to come to the College once a term to attend the Stated Meeting of the Governing Body at a specified time. An examination of the attendance record for a later period found the average turnout was forty-four per cent among the Visiting Fellows. Nuffield tried to encourage them to *'take an interest'* in the College's *'conduct, research and activities'* and it suggested this could be accomplished by providing for the development of a *'closer link between those engaged in research in the College and those engaged in practical affairs'*. It is unclear just how many Visiting Fellows were diligent enough to respond to that suggestion in practice.

But the College in the 'golden years' was well regarded by outsiders who came to Nuffield as its guests. The young Anthony Wedgwood Benn, a friend of David Butler since their undergraduate days at New College, recalled with enthusiasm in his diary for December 1957 a visit to the College to perform at a politics seminar. *'It has absolute equality between men and women and close camaraderie between teacher and student. It draws its fellows from a wide social background. There is no snobbery about it at all'*. But by 1978 when he was now just plain Tony Benn, he was far less impressed by what he found on a visit to a Butler seminar. *'The Nuffield academics live somewhere between big business, the mass media and the ivory towers of academe. They are cynical, detached and are only impressed when others are impressed. They respond to the events of political power and strength but they themselves never really move.'*

To Bill Rodgers, the Labour MP for Stockton-on-Tees and future Cabinet minister, Nuffield College in 1973 had achieved for itself an essential and integral place in the career projection of the life of the professional politician. *'The career for the ambitious young man is plain – a reasonable degree in philosophy, politics and economics, a year or two at Nuffield College Oxford, a period as a trade union research secretary, secondment to government or one of their outposts dealing with pay and prices, speech writer to Lord Kearton (then from Courtaulds) and perhaps a job in Brussels'.* Perhaps Rodgers had in mind his own research assistant Roger Liddle, who had worked for Bill McCarthy on industrial relations. Liddle was later a member of Tony Blair's Number 10 Downing Street policy unit and a functionary in the European Commission. A number of former Students did become Members of Parliament. They included Fred Mulley, Brian Walden, Austin Mitchell and Stanley Henig for the Labour party. Alan Beith, a Student in the 1960s, has been a Liberal Democratic MP for over thirty-five years. William Wallace of the same party was made a Liberal Democrat peer, along with Matthew Oakeshott, who was once Roy Jenkins's research assistant and is now an effective Treasury shadow spokesman in the House of Lords.

Nuffield in its 'golden age' was the scene of many glittering public occasions. At one famous Feast held in the College in February 1965, the guests at Chester's High Table were especially impressive. Labour Prime Minister Harold Wilson was driven over from Chequers for the event. The dinner was also attended by Jim Callaghan, the Chancellor of the Exchequer. Edward Heath, the soon to be elected Conservative party leader was present as well as Jean Monnet, the first chairman of the European Commission.

Some Fellows can also still remember the High Table in College that was held on 19 March 1963 when many of the country's leading trade union leaders were dining with the Fellows. It was the night that Warden Chester announced to the assembled gathering that the radio had just announced Labour party leader Hugh Gaitskell was dead. After a rather perfunctory bout of condolences, according to witnesses, the trade union leaders proceeded to denounce politicians in general and trumpet their own self-importance. Some former Fellows also remember a High Table Dinner in November 1963 when Max Beloff rushed in to tell them that President Kennedy had just been assassinated.

Such memorable public occasions during the College's 'golden age' were strengthened by the emergence of strong informal and personal networks of influence between Fellows in the College and senior figures in government departments, the national media and Parliament who came to Nuffield as Visiting Fellows.

The College gained a certain public notoriety in the 1962-1963 academic year when economics Fellow Ian Little, on the advice of his friend Tony Crosland, Labour MP for Grimsby, organised a series of tutorial seminars for Jim Callaghan, who was then shadow Chancellor of the Exchequer and a Visiting Fellow in the College. *'I assembled a group of Oxford economists who had all been members of the economic section of the Treasury'*, Little recalled in his privately published memoirs. *'I suspect I imposed this condition to keep out Thomas Balogh who would, I thought, sabotage the quiet rational discussion of economic issues which Crosland and I had in mind.'* Little recalls they all met with Callaghan in the College only in total about half a dozen times and he does not believe the seminars were particularly valuable to either side. As Little recalled the main topics they discussed were demand management, exchange rate policy, devaluation and prices and incomes policy. *'I do not know whether these sessions helped Jim'*, recalls Little. *'I thought he tended to steer the argument into political channels before all the economic issues had been fully explored. One thing seems certain. We did not convince him that devaluation would not be a discreditable and shameful measure. In September 1963 I disappeared to Africa for the Michaelmas term and the seminars ceased. I never discussed economics with Jim again.'* Later, when Callaghan was Home Secretary, he became the object of some militant criticism from some Students when he visited the College, to the anger of the Warden. Callaghan's blunt refusal to recognise the British citizenship rights of Kenyan Asians who carried British passports aroused deep emotional feelings at Nuffield, not least from Ian Little. This author remembers Callaghan having to face public protests in the quadrangle from Students over the whole shabby affair.

Politics Fellow Philip Williams composed a short poem that reflected the buoyant mood of the 1960s when it often seemed that Nuffield had turned itself into one of the centres of Labour's ruling elite:

> Some Fellows run the government, commuting up and down
> To London – though a few of us stay here to run the town
> There's Fellows on the BBC pronouncing on the news
> And Fellows of the Sunday press who phone in their reviews.
> And George would like our counsel wise on how to handle Jim
> And Jim is also to us for we're advising him.
> Our several economists have answers to supply
> If they only knew the questions. But we haven't DDI
> There's Fellows on the telephone from morning until night
> Yet one or two eccentrics still prefer to read and write
> And grab at the detested thing with irritable snort
> When its loud insistent jingle has derailed a train of thought.

The relevance of the College to the world of the swinging '60s was confirmed on 19 May 1963 when the Atticus column of the *Sunday Times* was entirely devoted to a glowing and entirely uncritical portrait of Nuffield and its position and status among Britain's ruling class. The College was described as a *'precocious power house of ideas which will have a potent hand in the policies reshaping the country whichever party is in power'* Atticus believed that the College was inhabited by the kind of self-important and serious minded men (and they were all men) who could be found in the stodgy pages of a C P Snow novel. It suggested that Warden Chester was virtually synonymous with the College *'The informal atmosphere with Students and Fellows on Christian name terms probably springs from him'*, Atticus suggested. *'There is no other College, least of all in Oxford where the dons naturally gather in the Junior Common Room for coffee after lunch or afternoon tea rather than go to their own Common Room.'* The *Sunday Times* noted the apparent egalitarianism of the College. It quoted the Warden as saying; *'I am sorry for people with a working class chip on their shoulders. If a man went round telling everyone he went to a public school they would think he was daft. So why should anyone go around saying he went to an elementary school? It's what you've done yourself that matters'*.

Atticus was invited for a dinner with the Fellows on High Table one evening. His description of that occasion evokes Nuffield's heady atmosphere of 1963: *'The dinner started at 7:15. The conversation was the sort of high powered shop which is only possible when at least six experts can pick holes in each other's ideas. But after the crème Portugaise, the quiche Lorraine, the braised duck Moliere, the praline ice and cherries plus two wines we retired to one of the Senior Common Rooms where another table was all laid.*

Stage two was "dessert" plus three wines (vintage port, hock and Madeira) but as the dessert consisted of a dozen different types of fresh fruit, glazed fruit and nuts, it seemed like another meal. The conversation was then becoming a little looser though still indirectly shop. "Did you know," asked one Fellow "that school masters are the least fertile of any white collar group?"

Stage three meant a lift journey ten floors up to the other Senior Common Room in the College Tower where coffee and liquors were waiting. "I'm used to a society based on sex", said one young Fellow, recently arrived at Nuffield from Birmingham University, "Now I'm getting to know one based on gluttony". [Chelly Halsey admits that it was him although he was unnamed by Atticus at the time].

It was approaching eleven o'clock and the gathering was beginning to thin out. I was told by one Fellow that it was at this stage that the really important guests were invited by the Warden to join him at table tennis. (Watch his back hand I was warned.) The invitation came but I was soundly beaten 21-15. After table tennis the dinner was over'.

Chester was never entirely comfortable with such close media attention to the College, however favourable and uncritical it usually turned out to be. *'Nuffield is sometimes thought to have much more influence than any academic institution can ever possess'*, he wrote later in the *Oxford Magazine* in 1971. *'To be called a power house is flattering but absurd. If the politicians, civil servants and others who have to make public decisions gain something from discussing current issues in the College, all well and good. We on our part certainly benefit – it is stimulating to have to match academic theory with practical problems.'* Chester pointed out that most of the permanent Fellows had at one time or another enjoyed a spell in the higher reaches of the civil service or as a senior adviser to the British or some foreign government. He believed the problem this posed to the College was *'not how to create links but how to retain the measure of aloofness necessary for an academic judgement'*. Chester was really rather ambivalent or perhaps he was just a little muddled about what he thought the ideal relationship ought to be between the College and the outside world of the policy makers. But it was almost always impossible to secure a balance, let alone often to reconcile the College's different purposes as an eminent academic institution with a high reputation for scholarly excellence, with its strong commitment to securing an active engagement with the outside non-academic world.

Hugh Clegg and the 'Oxford School'

Under Chester's benign but firm direction during his years as Warden, however, a number of the College Fellows proved to be relatively successful in bridging that perceived gap between academia and the world of public policy making.

One of the most important figures in the College in that respect during its 'golden age' was Hugh Clegg. Between his election to a Nuffield Fellowship in 1949 after two years spent as a College Student, until his move in 1966 to a Chair at Warwick, soon becoming the head of its newly formed Industrial Relations Research Unit, Clegg exercised enormous influence and authority inside the College. He had been a leading organiser of Norman Chester's campaign for the Wardenship. The two men shared a common belief in the empirical and the institutional. There was also a temperamental affinity between them as they worked amicably enough together on the necessary chores of College administration. It is no surprise to learn that some Fellows wanted Clegg to succeed Chester on his retirement in 1978.

Under Clegg's direction Nuffield became the leading centre for the academic study of industrial relations in Britain. In the 1960s the College was the focus for what was loosely defined as the 'Oxford School', with its clear and distinctive commitment to the so-called voluntarist tradition of industrial relations, based on a deep scepticism about the use of statute law or any resort to state intervention in the shaping of workplace attitudes for workers, trade unions and management. Clegg used to declaim that *an ounce of fact was worth a pound of theory but much more difficult to come by*. He also agreed with his close associate Bill McCarthy that the 'Oxford School' sought to ensure *something we say somehow must be of use to someone some time*. Clegg cultivated an apparent distaste for ideological approaches to industrial relations. He used to call himself a historian and not an economist or a sociologist. A Communist in his youth, Clegg never joined the Labour party but nobody could doubt where his sympathies lay. In his interview for his Nuffield Fellowship Chester asked him whether he was still a Communist and was no doubt relieved to hear that he was not. Clegg believed more in the case study approach to the study of industrial relations rather than the use of vast statistical surveys carried out by collaborative research teams. His early books included a volume on the General and Municipal Workers union and another on industrial relations in the nationalised industries. He later wrote most of a three-volume history of British industrial relations from 1889 to 1951 which was funded by a substantial grant from the Leverhulme Trust. His book, *The System of Industrial Relations in Great Britain*, originally published in 1953, became an indispensable textbook for students over a generation. It was revised in 1970 and again in 1979. Despite his public disdain for theory, Clegg also wrote a short and pithy book in 1976 that argued trade union structures reflected the structures of the collective bargaining systems they had to work with. Despite their insistence on a pragmatic, fact-driven empiricism as the Oxford 'school' approach, the claim was overdone. As McCarthy, later a College Fellow in industrial relations, told Brian Harrison in an interview, *There was idealism behind the pragmatism. We believed in collective bargaining and trade unionism – if workers wanted social justice they needed a union. We were in the business of facilitating the growth and development of strong trade unions*. Clegg and his colleagues did not deny the problems of unofficial strikes, the poor utilisation of labour and the dangers of wage push inflation to the economy. They wanted, however, to channel conflict in the workplace into more productive practices.

Clegg claimed that the collegial structure of Oxford University had helped to develop industrial relations as an academic subject at Nuffield. The lack of any industrial relations department and the diffusion of activity through a number of different institutions meant *'you could get bits and pieces here and there and put together something which nobody ever intended to happen'*. With no undergraduate teaching and no administration it ensured that the 'Oxford School' of industrial relations was regarded as somewhat peripheral to the University and this was helpful to Clegg too. But he also recalled having to face *'the total indifference, incomprehension and hostility'* towards industrial relations that was displayed by the University authorities in the 1950s and 1960s. *'It invoked a 'we'll show the buggers' attitude among us'*, he admitted.

Clegg, more than most other Fellows in the College, reached out deliberately to the real world beyond academia. *'Our reference points were outside the University'*, he told Brian Harrison. *'Without them we would have sunk without trace because our morale would have been non-existent.'* He was a close friend not only of many national trade union leaders but also industrial conciliators such as Sir Jack Scamp and Sir Richard O'Brien. It was the practical, no-nonsense side of Clegg that appealed to Chester's own down-to-earth vision of the purposes of the College. He ensured that a steady flow of important national trade union figures – George Woodcock, Frank Cousins, Jack Cooper, Bill Carron, and briefly Les Cannon – came to the College over the years as Visiting Fellows or as his regular guests. They attended dinners but also participated in conferences and seminars organised by Clegg. His own Thursday afternoon industrial relations seminars became an important feature of Nuffield's academic timetable and attracted many adult working-class students from nearby Ruskin College who had already considerable hard experience of shop-floor life, mainly as trade union activists. From the middle of the 1950s Clegg was appointed regularly by Governments, both Conservative as well as Labour, to take part or head important public inquiries into vexatious industrial disputes and other labour relations problems. He brought to them his known reverence for facts and his close attention to detail in finding solutions or negotiating settlements. Clegg's most important intellectual influence was undoubtedly on the final report from the Donovan Royal Commission on trade unions and employers' associations, that was published in 1968. As Pat Thompson, a close friend and historian at Wadham College, reflected, Donovan *'was Clegg's greatest success. He was largely responsible for its massive research and by threatening a minority report, inveigled his colleagues into abandoning any suggestion of legal restraints on trade unions in favour of trying to improve collective bargaining through consent and co-operation'*. Clegg's arguments were to form the core of the Donovan Report's recommendations. But while its modest and sensible proposals may have reassured trade unions and modified the attitude of employers, they seemed frustratingly timid and insufficient for impatient government ministers such as the then Employment and Productivity Secretary, Barbara Castle, who wanted to do something much more radical and decisive about what the government regarded as irresponsible trade-union power. They believed the behaviour of the trade unions and their archaic structures were mainly to blame for the constant outbreak of unofficial strikes, restrictive employment practices holding back a productivity breakthrough, and ineffective management of the workplace. Clegg was also made a member of the Labour government's Prices and Incomes Board in the 1960s where he helped to administer the Government's prices and incomes policy. Later he chaired the short-lived Pay Comparability Commission in 1979-1980. This body was established belatedly as a Government initiative after the trade union struggles of the 'Winter of Discontent' had destroyed its five per cent pay limited incomes policy. After awarding substantial wage increases for low-paid public service workers, the Clegg Commission was abolished by Prime Minister Margaret Thatcher a year into her government.

Clegg attracted a number of other scholars to work with him in Nuffield College who were loosely associated together in what is perhaps misleadingly described as the 'Oxford School', a term that he and his close colleagues were always sceptical about using to describe their general approach to industrial relations. The most distinguished of them was Allan Flanders, who was actually a genuine and original thinker of industrial relations, belying the widely-held view that

Nuffield's focus on labour questions was unashamedly empirical and untheoretical. As Richard Hyman, now at the London School of Economics and a Nuffield Student under Clegg's supervision, before going with him as a colleague to Warwick University, has reflected, *'More than any of his contemporaries in his area of study Flanders was notable for combining empirical knowledge with theoretical insight. His analytical arguments were also informed by his political principles. He insisted that industrial relations was a matter not just of income distribution but of rights and human dignity'*. It was Flanders who argued that while trade unions were economic institutions they also wielded swords of social justice in their activities. He, like Clegg, was to have a profound impact on the Donovan Commission. In 1967 Flanders wrote an essay for its members in which he argued that the *'largely informal, largely fragmented and largely autonomous'* system of industrial relations needed urgent structural reform to ensure that trade unions and management could *'pursue areas of common interest'*. Flanders recommended the creation of an independent permanent Commission on Industrial Relations (CIR) that would provide an institutional support for the proposed reform programme, through the use of plant-based studies of best and worst workplace practices. He served on the CIR when it was formed in 1969, but two years later the body became one of the casualties of Edward Heath's government, which took a more rigorous approach to trade unions, as exemplified in the 1971 Industrial Relations Act.

The other important figure in the College who specialised in industrial relations was Alan Fox. He had first come to Clegg's attention as an adult student at Ruskin College. He was chosen by him to write an officially commissioned history of the Boot and Shoe Operatives union after he had completed a study of industrial relations in the Black Country. In 1950 Fox became a Student at the College and went on to secure a Research Fellowship in order to co-operate with Clegg and Pat Thompson in the Leverhulme-funded project on the history of British trade unionism since 1889. Unlike Clegg, however, Fox moved steadily from a fact-based approach to industrial relations into the study of industrial sociology. In 1963 he secured a university lectureship based at Barnett House – by now Oxford's department of Social and

Administrative Studies – under A H Halsey's direction. In an appreciation of Fox in the *New Oxford Dictionary of National Biography*, Halsey noted that he began *'with a standard if enthusiastic commitment to the trade unions within an industrial relations system which produced low wages and long hours for the proletarian majority in a rigid hierarchy of status and conditions'*. But by the early 1970s Fox had grown more radical and critical in his analysis, and had begun to question the pluralistic assumptions of his former colleagues in the 'Oxford School'. His important volume, *History and Heritage: The Social Origins of the British Industrial Relations System*, was published in 1985. As Halsey noted, its sociological and historical analysis *'confirmed his position as the outstanding interpreter of industrial relations in the Britain of his generation'*. But it also amounted to a powerful criticism of Clegg's pluralism.

Clegg's successor in industrial relations at Nuffield after his departure for Warwick University in 1966 was Bill McCarthy. A mature student from Ruskin and graduate of Merton College, McCarthy wrote an influential thesis on the closed shop in British industry under Clegg's supervision. He was made research director to the Donovan Commission and then became an adviser to Barbara Castle at the Department of Employment and Productivity in the late 1960s. McCarthy was partly responsible for her controversial and ill-fated attempt to legislate industrial relations reform in the face of bitter trade union resistance. But for the most part he articulated the College's pragmatic tradition of combining public policy networking with academic research well into the 1980s although he did so with gradually diminishing influence and mounting despair at trade union decline. McCarthy was made a Labour life peer in 1975. McCarthy and his wife Margaret frequently attended TUC and Labour party conferences. He was able to move with what seemed like effortless ease and with some positive effect between the academic world and that of practical men. McCarthy was also a regular sympathetic champion of the trade union interest on a number of public bodies, most notably British Rail's arbitration and conciliation machinery.

Another important academic of industrial relations who also flourished under Clegg, both in the College and later on at Warwick

University where he succeeded Clegg as head of the Industrial Relations Research Unit, was the Canadian George Bain. He carried out a pioneering research project into the growth of white-collar trade unionism in the 1960s when at the College as a Student and then a Research Fellow. Later Bain became the head of the London Business School and then Vice-Chancellor of the Queens University in Belfast. He is seen as a shrewd, hard headed survivor from the age of trade union power and as such he has become an effective figure in the implementation of New Labour government policies. Bain was particularly successful as the first chairman of the independent Low Pay Commission that made recommendations each year on the level of the national minimum wage. He was later to incense the Fire Brigades' Union in a tough report he wrote for the Government that critically questioned the archaic customs and restrictive labour practices of their members.

Eric Batstone was a Fellow in industrial sociology at the College who died at a tragically young age although he had already established a growing international reputation for the quality of his scholarship. He came to Nuffield from the Warwick Industrial Relations Act, after carrying out ground-breaking fieldwork, on shop steward organisation and the complex relationship between management and shop-floor activists. As George Bain admitted at Batstone's memorial service, his empirical findings undoubtedly appealed to the prejudices of the 'Oxford school' because they confirmed their well-entrenched view that employee effectiveness in collective bargaining usually meant employee incorporation into managerial processes. An industrial anthropologist, Batstone used case studies in his researches but he was also prepared to apply theory to his work.

Batstone's sadly short life as a Fellow at Nuffield reflected the changing nature of industrial relations as an academic subject in the College. The clear shift in emphasis to workers and their shop-floor organisations reflected a radicalism that was at odds with the older concerns with the activities of full time union leaders and the corporatist tendencies of the 1960s. In fact, the most devastating critique of Nuffield's 'Oxford school' came from one of the College's sociologists. John Goldthorpe wrote a trenchant *'critique of reformism'* in which he challenged the conventional wisdom about workplace organisations and sought to argue that the massive industrial unrest and disorder of the 1970s reflected an intransigent workplace culture which rejected accommodation and compromise. Goldthorpe's prescient analysis exposed the increasing fragility of an industrial relations system that was coming under intense strain in the face of the pressure from inflation on workers' living standards. He drew attention to the consequences of a competitive fragmentation between workers in what many observers feared was becoming a Hobbesian struggle of all against all. In a joint project with Fred Hirsch, a fertile College Research Fellow who also died too young, Goldthorpe examined the social consequences of inflation and drew attention to what he defined as a 'mature' working class in the 1970s, whose militancy and sectionalism seemed to threaten any central attempts by the state to impose or negotiate order and stability. Like everybody else Goldthorpe had not reckoned on the return of a Conservative government led by a resolute Prime Minister who was prepared to challenge workers and their trade unions, even at the risk of tolerating a huge rise in unemployment to discipline pay bargaining. The set-piece industrial confrontations of the early 1980s were to confound what remained of the 'Oxford school' but also the more militant critiques of those who rejected voluntarism.

Nuffield's Politics of Pragmatism

The politics side of the College could also claim to have made a considerable impact during Nuffield's 'golden age'. Philip Williams made a particularly effective contribution. He was one of the few Fellows who was unmarried and actually lived in the College. *'A model of an Oxford don'* was how he was described at the memorial meeting held to celebrate his distinguished life at the British Academy. *'His College was his home and he treated it as such, comfortably moving about quadrangles and passageways in slippers and less than well tailored attire, his cherubic and cheerful face invariably badly shaven; no cook but a much loved dinner guest; unable to drive a car but never short of a lift from friends, colleagues or their spouses. To that other Oxford stereotype the distant and lonely dweller within the ivory tower he bore no resemblance'.* It is not surprising that many Nuffield Students still remember him with fond affection. In his early years at the College, Williams' research was mainly concerned with the politics of contemporary France. He wrote a number of important volumes on both the Fourth and Fifth Republics and won particular acclaim on the other side of the English Channel among his French academic contemporaries in political science. Williams was also an enthusiastic student of modern American politics although he did not write anything substantial on that subject. It was under his encouragement that the College acquired the Mellon professorial Chair in American Government for the College. At the end of the 1960s Williams turned his academic attention away from modern France to concentrate on the task of writing an authorised biography of his political hero, Labour party leader Hugh Gaitskell. His affectionate volume finally appeared in 1977, mainly to critical acclaim although he was somewhat inhibited from giving full coverage to Gaitskell's colourful private life by the sensitivities of his widow Dora.

Williams was a staunch right-wing member of the Labour party for most of his adult life although he joined the breakaway Social Democrats in 1981. In 1960 he helped to form the Campaign for Democratic Socialism, the Gaitskellite pressure-group based outside Parliament that fought successfully against Labour's short-lived commitment to unilateral nuclear disarmament and, less successfully, for the party's modernization through the repeal of Clause Four of its 1918 constitution, that called for the public ownership of the means of production, distribution and exchange. Williams was also always a firm supporter of British membership of the European Common Market. A strong political influence on his thinking came from Tony Crosland, a life-long friend from their early undergraduate days together at Trinity College in the late 1930s.

Sir Lawrence Freedman, now Vice-Principal (Research) at King's College London, was a Student at Nuffield in the early 1970s. He recalls Philip Williams as a *'wonderful man with his extraordinary gift for friendship and a chortling laugh. He was always dishevelled with inappropriate shirts and ties that never quite worked. His room was one huge fire risk, entered through a corridor made up of old* Financial Times *and* Herald Tribunes *piled up on either side, mingled with numerous books. He warmed to anyone who shared his enthusiasm for the business of politics and his international network of correspondents and friends was extensive. The idea that the study of politics could be a purely scientific, even mathematical, matter appalled him. Politics was to be relished for its intrigue and its scandal as much as its principles and procedures'.*

The other important and substantial Nuffield figure in the politics group of the College is David Butler. More than any other Fellow in the College, except for Chester, his name has become synonymous with the first half-century of Nuffield's life. The *Sunday Times* in 1963 described Butler as *'young, handsome and dynamic with strongly independent and impartial opinions'*. He was the pioneer of psephology in Britain, the inventor of 'swing' in explaining general election results and the rediscoverer of 'Cube Law'. His slide rule became an essential and ubiquitous instrument for calculation on general election nights on television. Butler grew to be a recognisable public personality as a result of his forensic television performances during the 'golden age'. In doing so he helped to put the College on the map. Many Students fondly recall working for him in the television studios on general election nights in compiling the results.

It was R B McCallum, an early Nuffield Fellow but also a Fellow at Pembroke College who inaugurated what came to be known as the Nuffield election studies. He wrote an account of the 1945 general election with Alison Readman as his co-author, after encouragement from Lindsay. McCallum was a political historian, who had written a study of British attitudes in 1919 to the Treaty of Versailles. He had been appalled by what he believed to be the serious misconceptions of that period to be found in J M Keynes's *The Economic Consequences of the Peace*, and determined that there should be no repetition in 1945 of what had happened. McCallum believed if all the politicians knew that a serious, scholarly book on the general election would be published shortly after its end, they would avoid stirring up the kind of hysteria and distortions that had poisoned the 1918 general election results. Just demobbed from the army, the young David Butler volunteered a statistical appendix to the McCallum/Readman volume and followed it up with another one in the 1950 general election study that was written by College Fellow Herbert Nicholas. Butler went on to become co-author of all fifteen Nuffield general election studies published between 1951 and 2005.

But his most influential and scholarly book, *Political Change in Britain*, published in 1969, was written in collaboration with Donald Stokes at the University of Michigan in Ann Arbor. It upset some of the more traditionally-minded politicians, academics and journalists with its use of the latest models and quantitative techniques and methods derived from American political science, but it soon became a classic of its time. Unfortunately there was to be no direct and immediate follow-up to that work in the College. Partly as a result, the new University of Essex became the centre of more data-based and professional surveys of British general elections led, initially, by Ivor Crewe, who had been a Nuffield Research Fellow in the early 1970s. After a long and distinguished career at Essex, where he was Vice-Chancellor, Crewe is becoming Master of University College, Oxford. In 1983 work on the British Electoral Survey was resumed in Nuffield for a further fourteen years under the leadership of Anthony Heath.

Butler's life-long interest in the study of general elections covered much of the English-speaking world and he was a regular academic visitor in particular to Australia, India and the United States, to commentate and write up their contests. Many College Students of politics who were under Butler's influence moved to other universities where they also focused on the importance of general election studies and political data. One of them was John Curtice, now a Professor at Strathclyde University and one of the country's leading psephologists. Other notable graduates of the College with a lasting expertise in electoral studies during the Chester years include Richard Rose, Anthony King, Michael Pinto-Duchinsky and Michael Steed, an indefatigable, almost obsessive expert on local government elections.

'DEB [David Butler] *was an introduction to the real live world of politics'*, recalls Pinto-Duchinsky, co-author with Butler of the 1970 Nuffield general election study. *'To be taken under his wing was to be given free access to the great and the good and to party agents and politicians at all levels. To go with him to the annual party conferences was an eye-opener. DEB gave very practical hints about how to get access to what normally was secret.'*

Butler's weekly Friday politics seminars (still running after fifty years) became an important feature of the College's academic timetable and they influenced generations of research students. A regular procession of important mainstream politicians, including government ministers, would come down to Nuffield for a grilling as they revealed and explained some of the mysteries of real politics at the Butler seminars. *'Butler's programme of guests excited me, as it brought the study and practice of politics together'*, recalls George Jones, recently retired from a politics chair at the LSE.

Butler was also a conscientious thesis supervisor. He wrote his own D Phil in only fourteen months – a history of the British electoral system between the 1918 Reform Act and the 1940s. Some Students admit in their memories that they could be a little irritated by his constant nagging over how their research work was progressing to completion. *'Supervisors really have only one essential word of advice – "write" he would say.'* However, Butler was an inspiration for many Students, who were often unsure and insecure about their thesis topics and needed help on how to carry out their work at a time when too often they were left to their own devices. He may have aroused some disdain among more fastidiously intellectual members of the College, of which he was well aware, who thought his work was little more than a higher form of quality journalism. But this was always unfair. Butler may have grown (like others of his generation) increasingly uneasy and disenchanted with the mathematical and rational choice direction that political science as an academic subject began to take, especially after the 1960s, but some Students later grew to appreciate that his close attention to facts and data as forms of empirical evidence was more valuable than they had once believed. Unlike others, Butler has not reshaped his thoughts and work in line with the fickle currents of contemporary academic fashion. But he has always shown little interest in theory or ideology. When an undergraduate, his philosophy tutor Isaiah Berlin told him on one occasion that he was the most unphilosophical pupil he had ever encountered. And yet he has straddled with some effect the often wide and uncomprehending chasm of mutual mistrust and suspicion that began to separate academia and the public policy world after the 1960s. As Butler admitted in an interview with the *Sunday Times* just before his retirement in March 1992, he created for himself the best of all possible worlds. To one he brought a *'dependable solemnity'* and to the other an *'unusual worldliness and familiarity with the here and now'*.

Political studies at Nuffield were always necessarily diverse and it would be wrong to suggest that the Fellows in that academic subject were either a cohesive or like-minded homogeneous group during the Chester years, focused almost exclusively on general elections and the gathering and analysis of statistical data. In the early period, John Plamenatz was a rather austere and distant figure in the College as a Fellow in political thought and intellectual history from 1951 to 1967. But his two masterly and elegantly written volumes – *Man and Society* – that explored the ideas of political thinkers from Macchiavelli to Marx became classic texts. Other important works included his *Democracy and Illusion* and *Karl Marx's Philosophical Man*. A stylish and incisive writer, Plamenatz was also a positive intellectual influence on a number of Nuffield Students as a teacher and supervisor. One of them was Larry Siedentop, a Research Fellow and later Fellow at Keble College, who studied the period of the eighteenth-century Enlightenment and its philosophical enemies. Others included Norman Geras and Robert Wokler, who were both at Manchester University. Some may feel, however, that Nuffield was not really Plamenatz's spiritual home. But when he secured the Chichele Professorship in Social and Political Theory in succession to Isaiah Berlin in 1967 and moved to All Souls, his replacement was Brian Barry, who took political theory in the College in quite a new, more radical and contemporary direction. Barry was outspokenly hostile to an historical and textual perspective to political thought. He once derisively likened that traditionalist approach to *'rolling the classics round the tongue like old brandy'*. Barry introduced what he believed was a much more rigorous approach to political theory that went back to basic first principles and the uncompromising use of philosophical logic. He wrote the important volume, *Sociologists, Economists and Democracy* when a College Fellow. It was indirectly a tribute to the inter-disciplinary character of academic life in the College. Barry was succeeded in 1979 by David Miller, who has continued in this theoretical tradition. A prolific writer, Miller has shown a particular interest in concepts of social justice, writing well-received books on market socialism, as well as nationality and citizenship.

Another specialist area for the College's politics group in the 'golden age' was local government. This was a particular research interest of Warden Chester. Bryan Keith-Lucas, a College Fellow, was always a strong champion of the subject before he moved to a Chair at the University of Kent. He was succeeded by Jim Sharpe. Local government became an increasingly marginal subject for research later on in the College's life.

Neither Keynesians nor Neo-Liberals: The College Economists

The strongest and most influential intellectual group in Nuffield during the Chester years were always the economists. They made Nuffield at the time into what some outsiders believed was the most important economics research institution in Europe. *'It had the best research, the best students and the best teachers in economics'*, recalls Martin Wolf, Student from 1969 to 1971 before going to work for the World Bank. In the past, the College has been home to three Nobel Prize winners in economics – Sir John Hicks, in the earlier period, followed by Sir Jim Mirrlees and Amartya Sen. All of them helped to ensure that Nuffield secured a well-deserved international reputation for the high quality of its economic research. Many of their contemporaries in the College were also highly professional academics with global reputations, who pioneered new directions in more theoretical and mathematical economics, that were to make a lasting impact internationally. Moreover, in the best Lindsay tradition, many of them mixed academic with non-academic work and spent much of their time and energy employed by international institutions such as the World Bank, the International Monetary Fund and the Paris-based Organisation for Economic Co-operation and Development, or at the Treasury, the Bank of England and Britain's clearing banks. The interconnection between the College and the City of London has been a recurrent theme over the past seventy years.

Up to the 1960s economics as an academic subject in Oxford remained relatively under-developed, even primitive. As Christopher Bliss has written, *'The very brightest students at that time could go straight from a mainly undergraduate education and without much formal training make significant contributions to economic knowledge. That this was possible simply reflects the fact that there was then far less economics to learn before one could dip one's pen into the research ink well. Only two or three journals and a few books could be called required reading. The literature review that burdens today's Student was then a far lighter task. This is not to say that a price did not attach to the slack preparation for advanced study that too many received. One encountered all too often serious gaps of knowledge and sometimes sheer confusion'.*

But as Bliss argued, in those days the relatively primitivism of economics provided the able post-graduate Student with substantial opportunities to advance themselves. As he explains; *'Today the experienced scholar has learnt the hard way that what seems to be a great new idea is very likely not great or not new or neither great nor new. Those early workers had it easy. They walked among trees hung with novel ideas and concepts like ripe plums ready to be plucked'.* Bliss warns that such a view is, however, somewhat misleading. *'What they did seems easy only because they did it. Yet it is the case that the truly original thinker enjoyed a huge scope and freedom to map out new paths that is now rarely possible.'*

Donald MacDougall was perhaps the most skilful of Nuffield's applied economists in squaring the world of academia and that of practical men. He exercised a particularly important influence on College affairs. MacDougall was appointed to a new Readership in international economics at Nuffield in 1950, and became an Official Fellow two years later. He moved with apparent ease between the College and Whitehall in the best Lindsay tradition. During the Second

World War he had worked in the Admiralty's statistical division under Professor F E Lindemann. It is said that he advised Churchill's personal adviser that the Keynesian economic principles contained in the Government's 1944 white paper on employment policy were quite sound. MacDougall took part in negotiations with the Russians on German war reparations, and he attended the Potsdam conference in 1945 at the end of the Second World War. A Fellow of Wadham, he was the first economic director of the Organisation for European Economic Co-operation in Paris (later it became the OECD). In 1951 MacDougall was made chief adviser to Prime Minister Churchill's statistical section in the newly-elected Conservative government (taking two former Nuffield Students, Maurice Scott and John Fforde with him), and he fought successfully against the Treasury's attempt to float the pound under the doomed Operation Robot.

During the 1950s, MacDougall played an active role in College life. He devoted particular attention to the construction of the wine cellar. More importantly, he was put in charge of Nuffield's investment policy, in co-operation with his fellow economist in the College, Ian Little, after the College became free of direct University control in 1958. The two men helped to transform the College into one of the wealthiest in Oxford University during the 1960s, building up a shrewd investment portfolio and the selling off of properties. As Christopher Bliss recalls, *'In the College MacDougall is remembered as a genial colleague with a sharp mind'*. He believes that MacDougall and Little between them *'produced a record of outstanding success'* in their investment strategy for the College *'with a performance far better than the UK stock market and other Colleges where a comparison can be made'*.

But MacDougall's invaluable services were increasingly required in Government. In 1962 he was appointed to become the first economics director at the newly-formed tripartite National Economic Development Office, and took leave of absence from the College to carry out his task. Two years later he was made Director General at the newly-formed Department of Economic Affairs by the incoming Labour government under the ebullient if erratic leadership of George Brown. As a result, he resigned from his Nuffield Fellowship, left academic life, and joined the civil service, although he never lost touch with the College and was a frequent visitor, and later an Honorary Fellow. In January 1969 MacDougall became head of the government economic service and the Treasury's chief economic adviser. On retiring from Whitehall in 1972, he did not abandon public life but went instead to advise the Confederation of British Industry.

Ian Little, Official Fellow from 1952 to 1971 and then Professor of Development Economics in Oxford until 1976, enjoyed a long and fruitful career that was inseparably associated with Nuffield. Christopher Bliss has described him as a *'philosopher of economics'*. His major work, *A Critique of Welfare Economics*, was published in 1950. *'Little showed that welfare economic recommendations must be based in part on value judgements but that these judgements can be limited in scope, being confined to the distribution of income'*, notes Bliss. *'Nothing else as good on that topic has ever been written.'*

Little then moved into development economics, after paying a number of visits to India. He became a severe critic of the use of protectionism and centralised state investment allocation in that country, which he believed was arbitrary and probably harmful to India's economic growth. But as Bliss explains, *'Little knew that his case would never prevail unless a clear alternative could be laid out'*. This was achieved in collaboration with his colleague Jim Mirrlees. Together they established, through the OECD *Project Evaluation Manual*, a *'complete system of project evaluation based on mapping from international prices for tradable goods to shadow prices for all goods and factors'*.

Such pioneering research work helped to make the College an important centre for the growing movement in development economics. Bliss argues that the OECD Manual *'became almost the World Bank standard for project evaluation'*. The ideas that emerged in the College, he maintained, were called 'neo-classical'. But he argues that *'the term was often used then in a disparaging sense. Leaving aside the poor judgement involved in dismissing this approach, the ascription was not accurate. It is true that the new view treated developing countries' market economies and held that market prices are both useful signals and important incentives. However, with this view, came a real appreciation of the problems that flow from imperfect and absent markets'.*

Sir Jim Mirrlees is seen by many in the College as the most influential Fellow in economics during Nuffield's first half-century. He was Edgeworth Professor in the College for twenty-seven years, from 1968 until 1995. Christopher Bliss has written that his influence took two forms. *'As the supervisor of numerous talented graduate students, he set a standard of rigour and intellectual ambition that enthused more than a generation.'* Mirrlees was *'a powerful locomotive force in the reform and definition of the economics M Phil'*. Bliss has claimed that *'the community of economics teaching Fellows across Oxford colleges is dominated by people who owe more to the influence of Mirrlees than to that of anyone else'*. Mirrlees started as a mathematician before changing to economics under the influence of Champernowne. One of his greatest contributions to economics was his theory of taxation for which he was co-winner of the Nobel Prize in 1996.

Like Mirrlees, Aubrey Silberston moved to Nuffield from Cambridge in 1971, and he remained at the College for six years before moving to Imperial College, University of London. Silberston was an industrial economist with a special interest in the car industry. *'Although he used little high theory himself, he was always on the side of the angels, in the sense that he supported theoretical economics whenever it stayed connected with real world problems'*, writes Bliss.

Philip Andrews, an economist who seemed a rather solitary figure in the College during the earlier Chester years was, Official Fellow from 1947 until 1967, when he moved to the new University of Lancaster with his colleague Elizabeth Brunner. Bliss recalls that *'his somewhat isolated position owed more to a certain awkwardness of character and to poor communication than to weakness in his work'*. Andrews could be irascible and difficult. He found it hard to be collegial and he did not suffer those he regarded as fools gladly. Andrews was concerned with the economics of the private firm, which was rather an unfashionable interest in the 1960s. *'He believed in listening to businessmen and taking what they said seriously'*, writes Bliss. *'It is a potentially fruitful route but one littered with traps. The economist must absorb every scrap of information that his respondents offer him but never 'go native'.'* Andrews also wrote an officially commissioned and discreetly affectionate biography of Lord Nuffield, whom he greatly admired. *'He was much more successful than the subsequent influence of his writings might suggest'*, concludes Bliss. *'The world changed rapidly in the post-war years and an approach to the firm that owed much to the depression years soon became far less relevant.'*

Marty Feldstein was a member of the US Council of Economic Advisers during President Reagan's administration, and later professor of economics at Harvard University and president of the National Bureau of Economic Research. He was a Student, a Research Fellow and an Official Fellow at Nuffield during in the 1960s. Feldstein later spoke of his *'unique experience'* in belonging *'to a social science College with links not only to the University but also to the government and business community in London ... The combination of high quality technical economics in the seminar rooms and of stimulating debates about economic affairs in the common rooms and at High Table have left me with a permanent and pleasant impression.'* Bliss recalled that Feldstein was the first and perhaps the only Nuffield Student to have his own research assistant, though this is not strictly true, since Sir Roderick Floud claims he had a research assistant as well while a Student in the mid-1960s.

Another substantial intellectual force among the economists in the College in the Chester years was John Flemming. He was an Official Fellow from 1965 until 1980, and later became a senior and influential figure at the Bank of England and then Warden of Wadham College, where he died from cancer at a tragically young age. Flemming, Bliss recalls, was *'one of those rare individuals who are so bright that they make most academics seem slow-witted by comparison. Yet his gentle disposition meant that he never put anyone down directly. He would simply ask a question. Later, in this writer's experience, would come the realisation that the argument that one had been confidentially pressing on John was riddled with problems'.* Flemming's main interests were in banking and macroeconomics. *'He worked on consumption theory with imperfect capital markets long before that approach became fashionable'*, says Bliss. Flemming wrote a book on inflation that owed much to his daily commuting journey to London and his job at the Bank of England. As Bliss notes,

Flemming *'saw the slow queues to buy a rail ticket while the travellers paid by credit card as a rational response to rapid inflation which made paying up to six weeks later a serious consideration. Aside from the clarity and directness so characteristic of John's writing the book advertised the importance of inflationary expectations at a time when this concept was only just beginning to receive the attention it was to enjoy later'.*

Terence Gorman was professor of mathematical economics and a Professorial Fellow at the College from 1962 to 1967, after which he took up a chair at the LSE. In 1979 he returned to Nuffield as an Official Fellow for three years until his retirement. *'Gorman was an Irishman with a powerful individual mind'*, explains Bliss. *'He worked largely on his own with his own ideas. This is usually a recipe for obscurity and local acclaim at best. That it resulted in Gorman's case in world-wide recognition and widespread citation is to be explained simply by the great originality and outstanding quality of his work.'* Bliss emphasised Gorman's abilities as a teacher. *'He was dedicated to the highest standards and he always believed the young to be the great hope for economics. They had the time and the incentive to penetrate his heavy Irish accent and to decode his sometimes brief and obscure brilliancies.'*

Transport economics was a strong part of the discipline in 1960s Nuffield. Chris Winsten was an Official Fellow from 1963 until 1970, and was closely involved with Christopher Foster at that time in developing the Department of Transport Studies in the University. The other transport economist in the College was Denys Munby who was murdered tragically on a holiday in Turkey in 1976.

Max Corden was Nuffield Reader in international economics from 1967 until 1976. He wrote two important books on the subject during his time at Oxford. As Bliss has argued; *'Corden pioneered the treatment of non-tradeables in international economic theory'*. Another formidable College Fellow in development economics was Maurice Scott, who was a Fellow at Nuffield for twenty-four years from 1968 until his retirement in 1992. *'He started under the cost benefit analysis umbrella that has been a major stream in Nuffield economics history'*, writes Bliss. Later Scott examined the reasons for economic growth and the relevance of improved technology in that process.

Economic history was always a strong subject area in the College although Nuffield never appointed an Official Fellow in the subject. Its longest serving Professorial Fellow was Max Hartwell, who was at Nuffield from 1956 until 1977. In Brian Harrison's words he was *'unpretentious, approachable, funny and yet conscientious – a splendidly reassuring and balanced human being'*. An ebullient and forceful, some thought brash, Australian, Hartwell became a formidable protagonist in what during the early 1960s was a fierce controversy over working-class living standards during the early stages of the British industrial revolution. Hartwell confronted the fashionable Marxist views of the time, which asserted that workers and their families suffered severely from a sharp decline in their real incomes and consequent poverty and exploitation. This view was most apparent in the works of Edward Thompson and Eric Hobsbawm. Hartwell was actually well ahead of his time in his commitment to quantitative economic history, and he was able to argue that the fashionably pessimistic approach to the living standards issue ignored the other, more positive side of what was always a complex picture in early nineteenth-century Britain. In retrospect, Hartwell's trenchantly expressed but well-argued fact-based arguments stood up rather better than those of the Marxists in the living standards debate. In his emphasis on the importance and knowledge of free market economics in the study of history, Hartwell was well ahead of his time. Perhaps more than other College Fellows in economics, he was always an outspoken believer in the kind of neo-liberal economics that were later associated with Margaret Thatcher and Sir Keith Joseph. Hartwell was a member of the economically liberal Mont Pelerin Society and later became its historian. He also wrote some argumentative work for the neo-liberal Institute of Economic Affairs.

Hartwell was to be followed at Nuffield by three equally formidable economic historians, although they were to remain Fellows for shorter periods of time: Barry Supple (1978-1981), Charles Feinstein (1987-1989) and Avner Offer (1990-2000). Supple worked mainly on post-1918 economic history, while Feinstein continued his researches into the compilation of historical time series for the British economy. Offer brought a new focus on quality of life issues and consumption in economic history. The current Fellow of economic history in the College, Robert Allen, has widened his concerns to cover pre-industrial economic history and whaling.

Peter Sinclair, now an economics Professor at Birmingham University, and former Fellow at Brasenose, where he taught economics to the Conservative party's David Cameron, holds vivid memories of the College's economic Fellows when he himself was a Nuffield student in the late 1960s, working for his B Phil: *'Studying economics at Nuffield in that period was daunting. The College was the powerhouse of all serious economics in Oxford then – especially when you include Sir John Hicks at All Souls (former Nuffield Fellow), recently retired but still teaching and very active. It was not just that its Fellows dominated the intellectual scene. Just as important, the College was the stage for nearly all of the best 5pm seminars.*

On Monday it was industrial economics. Here you feasted on a rather odd diet of sceptical but informal empiricism about what really drives firms' pricing, investment, research, employment and financial behaviour. The highlight was often a trip to Cowley to see the decaying strike-prone and mismanaged legacy of the College's Founder.

Tuesdays or Thursdays – it varied – saw sparkling high brow debates on monetary and fiscal matters or rather the deeper concepts that underlay them. Debate was led by John Flemming who spoke like the most eloquent hero of a Tom Stoppard play. He was a river of ideas in spate, a torrent of clever one-liners that tumbled over each other, usually so fast that it was really tough to keep up. But John was extraordinarily kind to struggling students and would listen to our paltry arguments, hiding his impatience until intervening with 'Perhaps I might be allowed to try and put your point this way –'.

On Wednesday it was the turn of international economics. Here Max Corden led a big team. Vijay Joshi and Peter Oppenheimer were usually there, and sometimes the terrifying figure of Harry Johnson, making an unforgettable cameo performance — forceful, irate and controversial. But the central figure was Max. First he explained with a beautiful diagram what the speaker had meant to say. Then he questioned it. Finally he built an elegant model that really taught us how to tackle the subject, start simple, then add and add and add, but always keep it clear.

Some Thursdays saw Denys Munby talk or host a talk on transport economics. We thought out how we could improve on Dr Beeching or construct optimal fare vectors for buses or understand why Paris' poor, unlike New York's, lived on the edge. We knew Denys' heart was more in church architecture and socialism but that never showed in the seminars.

But the real high point came on Friday. This was the research seminar. It was run by Jim Mirrlees. Jim had inherited it from Terence Gorman. Terence was later to return for a glorious retirement at Nuffield. I remember Jim attending the new Students' party. He too was a young new face. One of us asked him, "Are you doing the M Phil?'" "In a way yes", he replied. When we saw him behind the lectern in the large lecture room next morning we suddenly realised he'd meant that he was teaching it – indeed, in a sense running it. Neither in his lectures nor his seminar was he always easy to follow. All his remarks were penetrating but some of them have taken me forty years to appreciate. We learnt much from Jim and saw how determined he was to raise our sights far above what he deemed the complacent literary waffle of PPE.'

Peter Sinclair also recalls the exchanges with economics Fellows over tea or coffee in the College's Junior Common Room. *'They had a different flavour. Ian Little, often sporting plus fours and a magnificent Havana, would enrich our naïve discussions with witty teasing paradoxes. And then with a great gust of laughter, he and Maurice Scott would then recall a Finance Minister in Indonesia or Jamaica who'd got into a hopeless mess because he hadn't taken longer term reactions of this into account. Kindly Francis Seton would watch us talk, then smilingly explain how many matrix algebra really could enable us to keep track of the subtler interactions we had, well there was no other word for it, ignored. Max Hartwell and Herbert Frankel would challenge our comfy, lazy Keynesianism with historical and logical insights that were new and unanswerable. If we came out with trendy nostra we'd got from Lord Thomas Balogh or in one of those extremely rare forays into the classroom, Teddy Jackson, and we happened to be on our own, any one of these five would quietly expose them to be nothing but muddle and wind.'*

Sinclair says that economics at that time outside the College or All Souls was *'dominated by Balogh and Jackson. It was they who organised the rejection of a new degree course in economics and mathematics. They had the time to plot and torpedo pretty well any proposal for raising academic standards. They could not follow the Little-Mirrlees Manual on project evaluation or Corden's work on tariffs or Flemming's arguments about tax but they treated them as personal attacks on the sad little Three Ps policy recipes they themselves had been plugging for poor countries 'public ownership, planning and protection'.'* So there were territorial divisions. Balogh, Jackson and the college tutors controlled PPE. St Antony's would do area studies at graduate level with their economics component. But for serious, postgraduate economics, it was Nuffield.

'Nuffield's economics Fellows must have thought us students so silly and uninformed. We were spoilt and not just in our fine living conditions but intellectually too. They, the Fellows, were very patient with us. They really tried to treat us as equals. They too were puzzled by the ever changing tensions, between macro and micro, theory and applied, long run and short run, incentives and justice, markets and distortions, positive and normative algebra and intuition.'

Sinclair notes that it was never possible for Nuffield economics Students to discuss their subjects with others in the College. *'Both politics and the then ill defined third estate (which embraced everything from imperial history and trade unions, to criminology, religion, Comte and Durkheim) dealt with subjects that charged no epistemological entry fee. Anyone could chat about them at meal times. Asymmetrically, non economists thought of economics as a private language. So anything deeper than talk about the Budget was deemed off limits at the table. Economists need to interact and the tacit ban on the converse made them seem furtive and aloof. Nuffield was multidisciplinary. But interdisciplinary it was not.'*

Perhaps this was inevitable with the growing complexities and sophistication of the social sciences. Nuffield has always liked to see itself at the cutting edge of new thinking, but increasingly the social sciences were becoming more fragmented; mathematically theoretical but also quantitative, and perhaps to those outside that particular discipline more opaque and impenetrable, with a language all if its own that too often seemed jargon-ridden and deliberately hostile to wider public discourse. Of course, the more sophisticated and intensive the theories, knowledge and application grew, the more difficult it was for the College, even under Chester, to find much of that elusive common ground to build up a successful inter-disciplinary approach. It was a genuinely serious problem for those who still wanted Nuffield to aspire to the fulfilment of one of its lasting purposes – to bridge the gap between academia and the world outside its walls. This was especially true in economics.

As Peter Sinclair recalls in his vivid memories, Nuffield economists were challenging the comfortable orthodoxies of the post-war years as mathematics and econometrics underpinned theory and practice. Their thinking was grounded in a sophisticated mathematical empiricism. Ian Little and other development economists were more conscious than others that much of the conventional wisdom about how poorer countries could improve living standards and secure growth made little sense in the real world of international politics and economics. It may be true that none of the economics Fellows forecast the turbulence of the early 1970s, as the post-war Bretton Woods world of fixed exchange rates, regulation and controls passed away. The return of mass unemployment to Britain in those years also came as a shock to most of the Nuffield economists. The sudden and intractable surge of wage-pushed inflation followed by stagflation added to the misery. Public spending seemed to grow increasingly reckless and the level of personal and corporate taxation more onerous on individuals and enterprises. But at least it was a former Nuffield Student, Peter Jay, later British ambassador in Washington, and Economics Editor of *The Times* and presenter of the television programme *Weekend World*, who influenced his father-in-law, Labour Prime Minister Jim Callaghan, to announce the end of the era of high public spending in his speech at the 1976 Labour party conference.

Nuffield economics in the 'golden age' attracted a number of brilliant Students who went on to distinguished careers both inside and outside academia. These included Sir Derek Morris, now provost of Oriel College and once chairman of the Competition Commission, as well as Chris Allsop, a one-time member of the Bank of England's Monetary Policy Committee. Sir Gus O'Donnell, Cabinet Secretary for both the Blair and Brown governments, also benefited from a stint at the

College, as did Nicholas (now Lord) Stern and Tim Congdon. The late Andrew Glyn wrote a number of radical books on contemporary capitalism as a Fellow of Corpus. Bob Bacon co-authored with Walter Eltis (another ex-Student) an influential volume on Britain's economic troubles that pointed in particular to the growth of public service employment as a factor in relative decline. What is apparent in this partial view of the College economists, both Fellows and former Students, is their diversity and rigour. It never made any sense to speak of a Nuffield school of economics. On the contrary, the sheer rich diversity of the College's economists has remained one of its greatest strengths.

Nuffield and Europe

Under Norman Chester's active encouragement the College took an early interest in European studies. In 1956 the Warden negotiated with the Ford Foundation for the endowment of a Fellowship in the College on European politics as well as a ten-year programme of research and conferences. Its first Fellow was Max Beloff, but he moved soon afterwards to All Souls. Uwe Kitzinger was to be the longest-lasting Ford Fellow. He recalls that European political studies in the Nuffield context *'remained essentially a small-scale operation which never involved more than four or five people at a time'*. In addition, a special relationship was developed between the College and the Fondation Nationale de Science Politique, which began in December 1958 with a conference on the Fifth French Republic's constitution. Regular get-togethers were held four times a year in Paris and Nuffield, in which Philip Williams and then Vincent Wright played important organising roles. On these occasions, academics from both sides of the Channel met to discuss common political problems that were of mutual interest. Chester was always a strong champion of this particular academic *entente cordiale*. But David Butler complained later that the conferences were too one-sided affairs because, with a few notable exceptions, the French academics who attended them showed diminishing interest in British politics. *'I have sensed a certain emptiness behind the very pleasant goodwill of the whole affair'*, Butler told the Warden. The conferences came to an end in the 1990s.

Through his media performances, which were enthusiastically favourable to British entry, Kitzinger helped to establish a high public profile for the College on the European issue after Britain applied to join the European Economic Community in 1962. Later in 1975 he co-authored a volume on the British referendum on EEC membership. Kitzinger also became the founding editor of the academic publication *Journal of Common Market Studies*. The Warden himself took the lead in Oxford in the European Movement when it campaigned for a 'Yes' vote in the 1975 referendum.

Kitzinger has noted that the Warden could *'look back favourably on his years of work in the College which sought to ensure that the practical interdependence between Britain and the new Europe would not be neglected in academic research'*. He himself went on to play an important role as President of Templeton College and in the development of management studies, in which Norman Chester also played a significant part. In addition, Kitzinger also spent some time as the head of INSEAD management centre in Fontainebleau.

Kitzinger believes that colleges like Nuffield are far more flexible and adaptable than slow-moving university authorities and departments, to provide the necessary dynamism for change. The freedom that a College can give to individuals to pursue their enthusiasms is not 'easily replicated' in University departments, Kitzinger insists.

European comparative politics became the specialism of another dynamic Official Fellow – Vincent Wright. He came to Nuffield in 1977 and remained at the College until his sad death twenty-two years later. Nevil Johnson wrote in the *New Oxford Dictionary of National Biography* that while he doubted whether Wright found the College *'a particularly congenial intellectual milieu, his appointment there was ideally suited to his temperament and scholarly interests. It gave him complete freedom to pursue his steadily widening research interests, to write as much and as often as he wished, and to devote himself wholeheartedly to building up the many intellectual contacts and friendships that he formed not only in France, but in other western European countries too, especially Italy and Spain'.*

Wright was a popular figure in the College and many Students hold fond memories of his remarkable abilities as a thesis supervisor, a crucial adviser on career prospects and a personal friend. It is not surprising his memorial service in 1999 attracted hundreds. A temporary marquee had to be set up over the College pond to accommodate the numbers at the reception that followed.

In some respects, Wright might not have been regarded as a typical Nuffield Fellow, calling himself a historian first and foremost. In his autobiographical essay, *The Path to Hesitant Comparison*, written a few years before his death, Wight said he had no regrets that his first degree in politics at the LSE had been dominated by history and the great texts of political thought. He even admitted that he felt genuinely sorry for modern politics students who had received so little grounding in those subjects. His doctoral thesis written at the LSE was on elections in the French department of Basses-Pyrénées during the Second Empire. *'In writing my thesis I explored and even discovered themes which remain central to my intellectual interests'*, Wright wrote in 1996. *'I also acquired a taste for detailed archival work which has never deserted me. Given the choice of listening to yet another lecture on rational choice or spending the time in the local archives I should not hesitate an instant.'* Throughout his life Wright admitted he enjoyed an *'abiding love affair'* with France. Much of his work on the administrative history of nineteenth-century France was actually written and published in French.

But Wright came to Nuffield as a comparative politics Fellow covering much of western Europe as well as the institutions of the European Economic Community. He took a special interest in Italy, and was appointed to a Chair at the European University Institute in Florence in 1980. It was in those years that Wright learnt to appreciate basic theorising and the use of new methodological research methods. His appreciation of the College was warmly felt. It has, he wrote, *'one final advantage for the scholar; it is imbued with an austere and remorseless work ethic and its financial means help to insulate it from a wider British university environment which is undergoing radical and damaging change'.*

Wright was conscious that Nuffield had what he described as a *'curiously distant'* relationship with the rest of Oxford University although it made a *'hefty contribution'* to it, producing many of Oxford's social science teachers, organising lectures and seminars and supervising many research students. Despite this, he acknowledged that the College cultivated *'its own sense of separateness'* and was as a result *'viewed with little warmth by much of the University'*.

Wright acknowledged that he benefited from other Fellows in Nuffield who were not specialists in politics. Being there, he wrote, has *'enabled me to work with economists, has provided links with the methodologically exacting sociologists and has provided the facilities for fostering collaborative comparative work'*. The Centre for European Studies, funded by the European Commission and with which Wright was closely involved suffered an unhappy history during its short life. But it indicated that the College was keen to widen and strengthen its focus on European politics. Wright took an academic interest in economic policy-making in the European Union, particularly privatisation projects. In his later years he worked on a major comparative research venture into core company executives.

His broadening range of academic interests did not make Wright any more sympathetic to new trends in political science, although it strengthened his belief in the relevance of comparative work. As he explained, thirty years in British and French academia as well as visits to other European countries and American universities had *'slowly transformed a historically-minded single country specialist into a prudent and inadequate comparatist and one under the pressure of institutional attachments and student pressure, is more sensitive to problems of methodology and the need for theory'*. But he retained in his words *'the eye of detail and the sensitivity to individual action'* required of the 'good' historian and this, he believed, inhibited him from being a pure comparatist. Typically, however, Wright said he could live with this tension which he described as his *'intellectual schizophrenia – to preach the need for comparative method, to practise timid comparison, to close my door in Nuffield on occasions and write history and to profit from the networks of colleagues and friends created and consolidated by both politics and history'*.

The Demand for Recognition and Status: Sociology at Nuffield

The College under Norman Chester was painfully slow in allowing sociology to come to Nuffield. David Butler recalls that in the 1950s Oxford University, including the College that claimed to be devoted to social studies, shared a *'guilty conscience'* about this omission. The American sociologist Norman Birnbaum was given a seven-year Research Fellowship at Nuffield but he did not make much of an impact. Butler recalls *'I don't think there was any conspiracy against sociology but there was just a general prejudice on whether the subject was really worthwhile. A kind of scepticism not an animosity'. 'Sociology was at best seen as a means of practical training for social workers, at worse a species of authoritarian and linguistically bogus hocus pocus'*, writes Jose Harris, who wrote her doctoral thesis at Nuffield on unemployment policy before the First World War. It was as late as 1962 before the University agreed, and then perhaps reluctantly, to introduce two optional sociology papers into the PPE undergraduate degree course. A B Phil in sociology was offered to graduates, but not until after 1965. It took until 2000 for the University to accept the creation of a Department of Sociology. Even in 2008 there is still no separate undergraduate degree course in the subject. Nor, it needs to be added, is there one in either politics or economics.

One of Nuffield's most influential sociologists, A H 'Chelly' Halsey came from Birmingham as a Faculty Fellow in 1962, moving on to a Professorial Fellowship 1978. The first Official Fellow in sociology, Jean Floud, was only appointed as late as 1962. Both had been LSE sociology graduates under the influence of David Glass and they specialised in the sociology of education. Floud remained at Nuffield for ten years before moving on to become Principal of Newham College, Cambridge, but she spent much of her time in the College as a member of the Franks commission of inquiry into the University. The Warden regarded Halsey as a potential trouble-making radical. Halsey recalls being walked round the lower quadrangle of the College three times soon after his arrival and told by Chester that a decade of silence from him would not go amiss. The Warden, like so many others of his generation, worried about the academic legitimacy of sociology, even though they recognised its arrival in Oxford was long overdue. But he also recognised that Nuffield needed to accept the subject's relevance as a respectable and increasingly important and popular academic subject in 'modern' studies. Oxford anxieties were compounded during the 1960s by the apparent association that grew up in academic as well as popular minds between sociology and Marxism, but this was something that made no headway among Nuffield Fellows. The Warden came later to enjoy Halsey's company or at least gave him what he recalls as *some kind of tolerated approval*. Chester made him Keeper of the College Gardens, supported him for election to the University's Hebdomadal Council and took him to football matches. He also became the Warden's partner in the annual bowls match at Nuffield Place against the staff and students.

Halsey was also an important figure in the University as director of the University's Department of Social and Administrative Studies. On the College's Governing Body he proved to be forceful, argumentative and persuasive. On one occasion he upset Chester by questioning the morality of Nuffield's corporate investments in South Africa and succeeded in forcing the Warden to back down over the issue when Chester realised that the majority of Fellows would not support his own position. Most of Halsey's prolific output was written at Nuffield. He was the Reith lecturer in 1977. Further volumes appeared on the rise and fall of the donnish academic profession and the history of sociology in Britain. Halsey also edited an invaluable volume, *Trends in British Society Since 1900*. As many as thirteen Nuffield Fellows wrote essays for its third edition that was published in 2000.

The other crucial figure in the development of sociology in the College was John Goldthorpe. He came to Nuffield from Cambridge in 1969 with an already well-established reputation, as he completed a co-authored and highly influential three-volume study, *The Affluent Worker*. An assertive working-class south Yorkshireman from Barnsley, Goldthorpe brought into the College an incisive commitment to quantitative sociological analysis, and in doing so he strengthened its already established reputation for unalloyed empiricism. It was mainly under his influence as well as that of Halsey that the College established a rapidly growing, international reputation for the rigour of its sophisticated approach to sociological inquiry, especially in the area of class formation and social mobility.

Goldthorpe says that Warden Chester *did not really understand sociology but if you did a deal with him it would stick*. Certainly it was during his last ten years as Warden that the subject began to blossom at Nuffield. This was due in particular to the success of the College's Social Mobility Unit, established in 1969. It was a year before Goldthorpe's arrival in the College that Halsey and Floud had applied successfully for a grant from the Social Science Research Council to carry out a new study of social and occupational mobility in Britain. This was a follow up to the work done by David Glass and others at the LSE nearly twenty years earlier. The initial financial support was followed by a further grant in 1970, despite some resistance among other sociologists. The project was assisted in its initial stages by Dudley Duncan from the University of Michigan, who brought the latest sociological techniques from the United States to the project. Clive Payne, John Ridge and Anthony Heath, among others in the College, collaborated in the project which became in Halsey's words *the major focus* of Nuffield's sociology group from 1968 to 1980. The data sample used was of 16,563 male resident voters in England and Wales aged between twenty and sixty-four. Women were excluded. Two substantial volumes were published by Oxford University Press, containing the results of the Unit's research findings in 1980 and 1981. The first concerned *Social Mobility and Class Structure*. It revealed, contrary to some popular assumptions, the tenacity of Britain's class structure. Despite the widening access to educational opportunities after 1945, Goldthorpe concluded in the study that there had been as a result *no significant reduction in class inequalities*. As he argued, those who believed in egalitarianism faced a difficult dilemma at the end of the 1970s. *If they fail to maintain pressure for policies directed towards the achievement of a more open society, then they must expect to see the inegalitarian tendencies that are inherent in the class structure progressively reassert themselves. The hard truth may to some extent be obscured – though not changed – in a period of high economic growth; but once the élan of such a period is spent it is likely to emerge more starkly than before. There is in effect no half way house; the only choice for egalitarians is whether they are prepared to relax their efforts and accept the real possibility that their ideal of a genuinely open society may actually recede or whether they are ready to continue the struggle for this ideal and recognising that the potential for class conflict is in fact the potential for the social change that they wish to see accomplished'.*

The social mobility studies *'put Nuffield on the map in sociology'*, says Goldthorpe. *'It was the first time the College had undertaken such a comprehensive project.'* The experience upset some Fellows who felt it was in conflict with Nuffield's more individualistic approach to social research. It was to pose a real problem when the project team hired a large number of research assistants and officers to work in the College on the social mobility data. Their physical presence in substantial numbers at Nuffield upset some of the traditionalists who feared sociology was advancing inside Nuffield at the pace of an occupying army and undermining the College's traditions and habits. Goldthorpe recalls how the social mobility unit research staff had to fight for equal status with Students in the College and on one occasion picketed High Table as part of their militant campaign for trade union recognition. But despite the doubts and hostility of some, there is little doubt that the social mobility project gave the College a distinctive edge in British sociology at the time, and an international reputation for its insistence on quantified methodologies. *'Before then Nuffield was not a place to do serious social research'*, claims Goldthorpe. After the social mobility project, the reputation of the College grew overseas, especially in Sweden, Germany and Holland.

Student Memories of Nuffield

The College under Chester in its 'golden age' has left many of the Students who passed through its doors in the early years with fond memories. Professor Martin Harrison, a Student and then Research Fellow, studied the relations between the trade unions and the Labour party, at David Butler's suggestion. He spent much of his academic life at Keele University, specialising mainly in French politics. Coming to the College with a first-class honours degree from Manchester University he found Nuffield *'an exciting place full of articulate people grappling with challenging issues and full of enthusiasm. The College was small enough for one to know everyone, Fellows and Students, and there were so many opportunities to seek information and try our ideas with other people, especially over coffee or tea – a crucial dimension of college life at the time. People were accessible and supportive. The College was very 'Oxford' yet not as weighed down with a surfeit of tradition. The numbers of Fellows and Students were still sufficiently small that one had little sense of inward-looking blocs or groupings that talked only among themselves. In all, Nuffield was a place where one had a sense of things happening in the social sciences and which had a wealth of contacts with the outside world'.*

From its very beginning the College attracted a steady and impressive intake of overseas students. Laszlo Peter was a refugee from Budapest and the 1956 Hungarian Uprising. *'After dark, dour, depressed Budapest, Oxford was a bright, cheerful place'*, he recalls. *'At Nuffield, I met kindness; people were helpful and gave me the benefit of the doubt concerning my slow progress far longer than anybody could reasonably expect ... I was starving for knowledge before getting down to write a thesis.'* Like most students, Peter was impressed by the College library. With a key for every student, it was open 24 hours a day so searchers after knowledge could spend the early hours of the morning amidst the book stacks in the tower. He was strongly influenced by the College in many ways. *'Nuffield acted for me as a vacuum cleaner. I learnt there elementary things: for instance that a College runs better if it is managed by academics rather than by administrators (later, London in this respect turned out to be a great disappointment), that the purpose of studying political ideas need not be to find the theory one approves; that liberalism and nationalism, although bedfellows on the continent in the nineteenth century, are fundamentally incompatible; that democratic government and good government are two different things; that you do not necessarily vote for a party you approve but for the one that was likely to do less damage than the others'.*

Karl Kaiser, a Student from West Germany in the early 1960s, contrasts Oxford and Nuffield with the *'world of anonymous mass universities of the European continent'*. *'A totally new academic environment opened up to me at Nuffield'*, he recalls. *'The ease with which one could seek contact and intellectual exchange with both Fellows and Students was a totally new and cherished experience for me. Except for those moments on amazingly quiet Sundays when people barricaded themselves behind their voluminous Sunday papers it was always easy to approach anybody with a question or start a conversation on an issue of academic pursuit.'*

His thesis supervisor in College was Uwe Kitzinger. As Kaiser remembers *'He took me along on speaking tours on the cause of Britain's joining the European Community as well as to Party Conferences to observe the debate on this issue. To discuss with parsons, old ladies and red faced farmers why they did not (in regrettably few cases did) want to join those strange people on the Continent, was an experience I would not want to have missed. Interestingly, many of the arguments I heard then can still be heard today when listening to or reading the euro sceptics of contemporary Britain.'* *'The working conditions for academic scholarship in the College were superb'*, Kaiser also recalls. *'Like countless scholars before I found it wonderful to step into the Book Tower at any time of day or night, read and write in the midst of book stacks, seek for more materials for one's pursuit or simply let one's mind wander when contemplating the spires of Oxford from a window high above.'*

Kaiser remembers warmly the importance to him of certain Visiting Fellows. He was impressed in particular by Edward Heath, who during his time at the College, was the Minister in charge of Britain's negotiations for entry into the European Community in 1962-1963. He was *'a dream connection for a graduate student working on British policy on European integration. I was deeply impressed by him as he repeatedly commented on the phases of British policy starting with the necessity to join, the intricacies of negotiating and the drama of French President de Gaulle's veto'*.

It was also at the College that Kaiser first met Richard Neustadt who encouraged him to move on to his own University, Harvard, after his time at Nuffield. The College *'provided the indispensable environment for my first successful steps into serious scholarship'*, Kaiser remembers. *'But equally important it helped me to get an understanding for British politics and foreign policy as well as Anglo-Saxon political culture which were crucial for my later activities in universities, the British-German Koenigswinter Conferences, of the German Council on Foreign Relations.'*

When this author was a Student in the late 1960s he remembers a substantial number of Americans were Students in the College. They included Frank Gannon, then researching British press coverage of Nazi Germany in the 1930s, who became a White House adviser in the final days of President Richard Nixon and helped in the ghost writing of Nixon's memoirs. In that memorable year, 1968, the College had two Czech students in residence who reflected the growing divisions within what was then an unhappy country, as the Prague 'spring' ended brutally with the military invasion of the Soviet Union and its Warsaw Pact allies in August of that year. One was clearly a supporter of the old Stalinist regime and the other, who went on to the United States, embraced the possibilities for freedom and democratic pluralism awakened by Alexander Dubček and others. Nuffield even had, in the summer of 1968, a Soviet academic historian on a sabbatical who was a loyal defender of the so-called Leonid Brezhnev doctrine that justified the use of force if necessary to uphold the Soviet Union's domination of Eastern and Central Europe.

To Nuffield Students in the 'golden age', the College resembled a luxury hotel. The University did not cater much for post-graduates at the time. Overseas students who had spent a year or longer in other Oxford Colleges as graduates used to complain about the lack of interest displayed in them. The modern historian, Cameron Hazelhurst from Australia, recalls life at Balliol for Melbourne University history graduates like himself, before his years as a Student and then Research Fellow at Nuffield. He *'discovered to my dismay a cramped middle common room, the compulsory purchase of meal tickets for ghastly food served in soup kitchen style, [and] no indication that the College had the slightest interest in what I was doing'.*

Certainly nobody complained about the material conditions the existed in the College during the 'golden age'. Accommodation was comfortable, spacious and of a high standard. *'It was a very exceptionally comfortable billet in which, if one lingered, one could quietly get fatter and fatter (all those meals)'*, recalls Caroline Harvey, now a Conservative member of the European Parliament. *'Most of the students in residence seemed to have almost no social life at all bar watching TV with other students late into the night ... At that stage D Phil students were still very much left to their own devices – it was sink or swim and many, after two years of studentship comfort, sank.'*

Nuffield enjoyed the early benefits of central heating when other Oxford Colleges still shivered in relative austerity. Students each occupied spacious lounges cum studies with an adjoining bedroom and a toilet and bath close by on the same staircase. *'The premises were over cleaned; floors were slippery with polish, brass gleamed, high table silver sparkled. The cuisine was a dramatic improvement on the horsemeat steaks and spam and nut cutlets off which we subsisted at Balliol'*, recalls Bernard Wasserstein, the historian. *'Unlike our successors today, squeezed into bed sitters, most of us had a set of rooms. We were provided with all kinds of luxuries including travel expenses, telephone and photocopying allowances, although a limit was finally set on free Xeroxing when one Student took over the machine and turned it into a 24-hour printing press for the Claimants' union.'*

What Wasserstein remembers from his days as a Student and then Research Fellow during the early 1970s is that the College was a *'temple of high seriousness. With its communal living arrangements, puritan work ethic and high moral tone, it brought to mind the kibbutz where I spent my 'gap year'.'* *'A problem with college life [in the late 1960s] was its sheer comfort'*, complains Michael Pinto-Duchinsky. *'Since breakfast, morning coffee, lunch, afternoon tea and dinner were all free, why venture outside?'* He remembers slipping guiltily out of the College to have tea in the town with Ronald Butt, then of the *Financial Times* who was researching in the College for his well received volume on the history of Parliament.

Brian Reading, later adviser to the Bank of England governor, an economic adviser to Edward Heath, and then on the staff of the *Economist* before forming his own economic forecasting company, recalls the 'sheer glamour' of the College when meeting dinner guests like Lord Beveridge and Tony Benn, *'Awe is the word I would use of my first impressions of the College'*, he recalls. *'The intellectual level was a quantum jump ... upwards and outwards. I was totally stimulated but still felt nervously inferior. But then Nuffield in was not just a College, it was a family. We played together, especially table tennis and croquet. I regularly played bridge with Norman Chester, very badly, but he was worse. I only won when partnering his wife.'*

George Jones, later professor of government at the London School of Economics, was equally impressed by the sheer 'luxury' of the College *'and all free for me on a state studentship – the voucher system of the day'*. He was also overwhelmed by the intellectual intensity of the College. *'Talk went on in rooms, over meals, in the common room and walking round the quad, at all hours. It was the first time I had encountered people from overseas, and I was intrigued to hear about their lives in other countries'*. Jones says he was stimulated by the various social science disciplines that he encountered in the College. Like others, he points to the legacy of a *'large and varied network of contacts, to whom access later was smoothed because of the Nuffield connection, and with an ideal model of an academic community'*. It certainly shaped his attitude to the social sciences *'It made me suspicious of theorising, jargon and number crunching for their own sakes, since those who indulged themselves in those practices at Nuffield appeared to provide little illumination to the problems they tackled.'* Jones is rightly appreciative of what he saw as the pride and efficiency of the college staff – the servants, the cleaners, waiters and kitchen staff, the gardeners and the odd job man. They were and still are a vital and under appreciated but integral part in the making of the College.

In some ways Nuffield during its 'golden age' came to regard itself perhaps arrogantly and uncritically as a dominant force in the intellectual zeitgeist. Its standing in the outside world at that time is well conveyed by Vernon Bogdanor, who was a Student from 1964 to 1966. As he explains *'I came to the College at the very moment when Harold Wilson's Labour government was elected, so ending thirteen years of Conservative rule. The atmosphere in the College was optimistic, heady even, stimulated by close relationships with Whitehall and Westminster. Talking to the economists at Nuffield, it was easy to believe that a Labour government would, by relying on professional economic advice, resolve Britain's economic problems and secure rapid and uninterrupted economic growth. Talking to the sociologists in the College, it was easy to believe that crime and other social problems would be cured by a government which relied on professional advice, and was prepared to use money to solve social problems. The political scientists were heavily involved in projects of reform. Stronger leadership from Number 10 through a Prime Minister's policy unit, the introduction of Select Committees in the House of Commons, larger and therefore it was assumed more efficient local authorities and a more managerial civil service – all this would prove a great contrast to the amateurism of the long years of Tory rule and would provide the institutional underpinnings for the brave new world of social democracy. Everything would be onward and upward ... The social sciences, so I thought, offered the key to the universe.'*

But within two years, once Bogdanor had moved to a politics Fellowship at Brasenose College, he grew rapidly disillusioned with the Nuffield ethos, especially when the pound was devalued in November 1967. He writes now that through the 1960s and 1970s *'almost every instrument of social democracy had been tried to regulate society and the economy. Most proved of little use. The theories of social democracy had, so I thought, been tested to destruction'.*

He went on: *'As the twentieth century came to an end, my scepticism towards the social sciences increased. In the 1980s Britain had begun to move towards the market economy, something which none of the progressive-minded economists at Nuffield seem to have predicted. Indeed, hardly anyone in the 1960s suggested that one of the main themes of the last part of the century would be the retreat of the state not its continual advance. The trade unions, seen at Nuffield as benign partners with the government in the search for economic improvement, had led Labour into a cul-de-sac in the late 1970s, whose most obvious and visible signs were the dead unburied in Liverpool, cancer patients sent home from hospitals in Birmingham and rats roaming amidst uncollected rubbish in the streets of London. In the wider world European Communism had collapsed under the weight of its own contradictions, something which none of the Nuffield social scientists seem to have thought was possible. In a number of European societies, in the Muslim world and the United States religion had made a dramatic re-entry to become a prime influence on politics, something again the social scientists of the 1960s had not predicted.'*

Bogdanor draws the conclusion that the social sciences to which he had been exposed in Nuffield *'had been too mired in the conventional wisdom of the day to be effective and indeed that one of the central themes of British life in the decades after the 1960s was the failure of the social sciences. Social scientists seemed less able than, for example, historians to escape the unarticulated assumptions of the age in which they lived. They were critical of everything except their own ideological preconceptions. They were caught within closed systems of thought. Indeed, politicians such as Margaret Thatcher and Tony Blair seemed much more open to new ideas and much more willing to revise the old than supposedly open-minded academics. The social sciences remained a stronghold of Old Labour and the post-war consensus long after it had been discredited elsewhere'.*

But Bogdanor also rightly observes that in his drastic reappraisal of the conventional wisdom, he has drawn some inspiration from what many Students and some Fellows in the College used to dismiss as *'snivelling empiricism'. 'It appeared that the only way to avoid being led astray by accepting uncritically the conventional wisdom of the age was to be found in a severe attention to the facts of the case even if the study of the facts led to the overturning of comfortable beliefs.'* He now admits that he has much more respect than he once had in the 1960s for David Butler's general election studies and to appreciate the force of his dictum that there was no point in arguing about ascertainable facts. Bogdanor cites the example of work done by David Butler and the American political scientist Austen Ranney in the College on the role of referenda in parliamentary systems of government. No doubt it was a *'tedious task'* in listing all the referenda held in history in democracies. *'In my younger days, I would have sneered at that as tedious fact-grubbing.'* But he now acknowledges that the conclusions drawn from the study – that democracies used referenda without becoming totalitarian states but also that they were used infrequently and did not become *'addictive'*. This meant that although Britain had held a referendum in 1975 to find out whether the electors wanted the country to remain a member of the European Community it was unlikely this would *'degenerate into a Swiss system whereby referenda were held on average every year. And so it proved. The referendum in Britain was to be an exception, not an instrument for regular use'.* It was, however, the device used to ascertain popular support for assemblies in Wales and Scotland as well as Northern Ireland and the mayoralty of London.

Bogdanor now admits he was wrong to look down on Nuffield as a *'haven of empiricism'* when he was a Student there. Now he fears that the College has *'gone too far in another direction – the direction of behaviouralism and rational choice. Both in the 1960s and today, Nuffield has not done enough to resist fashionable trends. Nor has it fought hard enough against the bureaucratisation of the universities and the research assessment exercise. It is too eager to be nice to those in power'.*

Another of Bogdanor's assertions is equally pertinent. Back in the 1960s he recalls that the College showed *'considerable interest in history – political history, diplomatic history, and social and economic history. Today, I suspect that history plays a much less prominent place'*, he concludes. *'I regret this. I have always agreed with the late S E Finer's view that without history political science is in danger of degenerating into* a priori *theorising.'*

Paul Addison, a Student from 1965 to 1967 and who spent his academic life as a political historian at Edinburgh University, has similar recollections. *'Nuffield was buzzing with all the intellectual and political optimism of the '60s'*, he writes. *'I happened to arrive at a moment when Oxford dons were running the country, or so it seemed. Some were in Harold Wilson's Cabinet; others were commuting between Nuffield and Whitehall. The economists, Thomas Balogh and Nicky Kaldor, were to be seen at Nuffield high table. Harold Wilson was still at the zenith of his reputation and there was much talk of Labour becoming the natural party of government. Meanwhile the social sciences seemed to be advancing by leaps and bounds in their methodologies and insights. The New Left – represented at Nuffield by Robin Blackburn and Gareth Stedman-Jones – were rediscovering and reinventing Marxism. Sociologists were exposing the class structure, social policy experts the sources of poverty, psephologists the explanations of voting behaviour. In Whitehall after the thirteen 'wasted' years of Tory rule, there seemed to be a partnership for progress between government and social sciences, with Nuffield as the bridge between the politicians and the academics.*

It was a brief moment, soon to end in disillusion.' But what he witnessed gave Addison the feeling that something similar had occurred in the planning of post-war reconstruction between 1942 and 1945. *'When my book* The Road to 1945 *was published, the Oxford historian Philip Waller wrote in a review that 'the wallpaper is very Nuffield'. He was absolutely right.'* Addison did not become, however, hostile to the social sciences after his Nuffield experiences. *'The College imbued me with a lasting and perhaps excessive respect for social scientists. They are, after all, not quite the sages or the wizards of social engineering which they appeared to be in the 1960s. But if ever I have cause to refer to social class or criminal statistics or the permissive society, I can feel the beady eye of the social scientist upon me, demanding that I define my concepts or clarify my hypothesis.'*

Bernard Wasserstein remembers the surprising lack of political consciousness in the College during his six years. *'Apart from a few long-haired left-overs from the heady revolutionary days of 1968, the students were not very politically engaged. One or two put on lapel badges in support of the two big miners' strikes of the early 1970s and when Jim Callaghan (as Home Secretary) came to visit there was some loose talk about throwing him in the pond but it was all theory, no praxis.'* Wasserstein found the *'predominant tone of Nuffield political discussions among those who considered themselves as left-wingers'* was a *'strange mixture of credulous faith in the libertarian possibilities of neo-Marxism and cynicism about the lamentably bourgeois tendencies of the British working class. As for those under suspicion of being right-wingers, they exhibited only the first, hesitant intimations of what we later came to recognise as the anti Keynesian counter reformation'.*

During Wasserstein's time the College, he claims, was *'passing through a mathematical phase. Economists, sociologists and political scientists all tried to wrap up their ideas in baffling formulae and equations. Even the historians, not officially a group but a few crept in under some other banner – in my case masquerading as a political scientist, found ourselves swept up in this tide when the founders of 'Cliometrics' Robert Fogel (later a Nobel Laureate in Economics) and Stanley Engerman, co-authors of* Time on The Cross *– a study of the profitability of American negro slavery, came to visit. Not much of this rubbed off on me at the time, though as the years have gone by*

I have gradually learned the heuristic value of quantification in historical understanding'.

By the end of Wasserstein's years in the College, it seemed the good times were well and truly over. He recalls the winter of 1973 when the Heath government imposed a three-day working week as he shivered in his great coat by candle light. *'Did it apply to us we wondered?'* More seriously, the huge expansion in academic jobs in Britain's universities was coming to an end. *'In the heyday of university growth in the late 1960s any Nuffield student could walk into his or her choice of half a dozen jobs at a good university',* he recalls. *'Many did so after a year or two as a graduate student and before completing doctorates. After 1973 that happy era abruptly terminated. Terms of trade in the academic job market turned in favour of employers.'*

The ambience of the College in its 'golden age' was certainly Social Democratic. To many observers, it looked like an unassailable citadel of right-wing Labour and Socialist revisionism, close to the political thinking of Tony Crosland and Roy Jenkins. But this was never to be the whole story. There were always those in the College, even among the Fellows but perhaps more importantly among the Students, who did not fit into that conventional orthodoxy. A number of committed Conservatives flourished within its walls. It is true that Nevil Johnson, the politics Fellow, was rather the exception in supporting Margaret Thatcher's Conservative party. He even became her constitutional adviser for a while. But there were a number of Students who supported the Conservative cause. Pinto-Duschinsky came to the College after writing an interesting analysis of the journalism of the third Marquess of Salisbury. A young survivor of the Holocaust in Hungary, he is now one of Britain's leading experts on the fraught subject of party political finance, and he was unrepentant in his backing for the Conservatives. John Ramsden, Professor of History at Queen Mary's College, London, became a prominent historian of the Conservative party. He wrote a doctoral thesis on the Conservative Research Department while a Student at Nuffield, and went on to write three substantial volumes about the party in the twentieth-century.

Gillian Peele, also a Conservative and a Fellow at Lady Margaret Hall, complained of the *'somewhat dreary Labourite consensus'* she experienced when she was a Student in Nuffield. Caroline Harvey came to the College while at the same time she was elected as a Conservative councillor for Cherwell ward on Oxford city council. *'I think those interviewing me were rather intrigued by this'*, she recalls. But she does not think *'the College or my fellow students ever quite got acclimatised to the fact that I was a Conservative councillor. They were much more used to people like Matthew Oakeshott (now a Liberal Democrat peer) who arrived in the following year and looked at that time all set for a career on the left. I remember one student asking how I got to meetings in the wilds north of Belbroughton Road. He remarked, 'I suppose you go there by taxi?' and was stunned when I explained that I bicycled everywhere'.*

But the apparently impeccable Social Democratic consensus in the College's 'golden age' was not always reflected in some of its general attitudes to social change. Despite its early and pioneering commitment to gender equality, women still found it difficult to secure Fellowships in the College. After Jean Floud, Nuffield was to have no permanent female Fellow for fifteen years. Moreover, the Chester years were hardly a time of liberation for women Students in the College either. Gillian Sutherland, a nineteenth-century historian at Newnham College, Cambridge, has some bitter-sweet memories of the College in the early 1960s. *'Nuffield was an institution that was affluent, a little self-satisfied and overwhelmingly male in actual personnel and style.'* She was only one of four women in a College Student population of over fifty. *'The chauvinist style was at its most pronounced among some of the economists who appeared to look on all non-economists as a lower form of life; and women as below that. It was, I suppose, a useful preparation for surviving in academic life at the point at which I entered it. But it didn't do much to encourage academic self-confidence at the outset.'* As a female historian, Sutherland feels that Newnham took far *'more interest in my work and the trajectory of my career'*.

Judith Marquand, wife of David Marquand the political historian and commentator, also suffered from the rather awkward attitude displayed towards women in the College when she was a Student there in the late 1950s. *'In the summer of 1958, Warden Chester held a meeting with the JCR to explain the arrangements when the College became fully residential. He explained to them all clearly to everyone's satisfaction until he stated that there was of course no question of allowing women students to reside in the college. I timidly said I must be very stupid bit I did not see why it should be out of the question. He went bright red and said 'You must be very stupid'. There was a shocked silence. When I returned to Nuffield in 1959 after a year at Harvard there was a woman's staircase.'* This actually lasted only a few terms before such segregation was abolished. There was a noticeable increase in the proportion of women students in Nuffield after the 1980s. Today more than half the College's Students are women. But there is still a long way to go before the College seems likely to overcome its current gender imbalances. It still has only four permanent Fellows who are women. It also ought to be noted that Nuffield has no permanent Fellows who are not white. Black students are also not noticeable in the College despite the impressive international intake of recent years.

The Social Democratic ambiance of the College appeared to come under at least a temporary threat from the revolutionary left during the late 1960s. Nuffield was not immune to the wave of student unrest that temporarily engulfed a number of universities in Britain and elsewhere in the world. Indeed, it was seen as a hot bed of subversion in Oxford along with Balliol College. This was well illustrated by Professor Hugh Trevor-Roper's chronicle in the *Spectator* (November 1968) as Mercurius Oxonminensis:

> *'Know then that the fanaticks here are but few and those fathered largely in two of our colleges, one old and one new, but both equally hideous; so true it is as the philosophers say that grace of body reflects grace of mind. One was Balliol – the other Nuffield. Lately founded by a hugely rich mechanick who thought thus to supply himself with ingenoise merchant factors. But alas! Twas scarce founded before it was colonised from Balliol whose then Master the late Lord Lindsay being inward with the founder cozened the old man into filling the place with young fry from his own spawning bed. Tis now peopled with neoterick tub preachers who dignify themselves with*

sesquipedalian names as psephologists, sociologists etc.; anglice agitators.

The trouble lay in the spread to other Colleges of a 'tribe of young fellows' 'who after having sucked in the rank vapour of those places have been planted out in more wholesome ground to teach those new fangled subjects which drowsy guardians have suffered to be added to our good old trivium and quadrivium and the sooner they are brought to order by lopping their tainted branches and spraying their stumps with a good drench of sound doctrine the better we shall all thrive'.

Philip Williams became the reluctant resident College Dean during that turbulent period. He found much of his time was spent dealing with the consequences for the College of the student revolution. As he admitted, *'Experience elsewhere suggests that graduate students, especially in social studies, often provide the leadership; we had better recognise that if trouble occurs anywhere in Oxford, it may well be organised from here.'* On sabbatical leave at Princeton in the summer of 1968, Williams received a particularly anguished letter from Warden Chester that reflected the official mood in Nuffield of those troublesome times: *'There you are in a quiet little backwater in Princeton while Paris burns physically and Oxford burns spiritually. Actually if one were not in Nuffield College or near the Clarendon building one would not know that anything was happening in Oxford. The four or five Nuffield activists on the Committee of 90 go about with a heavy conspiratorial air and from time to time rather unkempt young men are seen entering the College and making their way to Trevor Munroe's room. However, I gather they are suffering somewhat from the disease which affects most left-wing movements – they are becoming a group of deviationists with some of their political theories getting rather rarefied'.* It is interesting to note in the 2008 College Newsletter it was revealed that Trevor Munroe has gone on to pursue an impressive academic career in the West Indies.

In the circumstances, Chester was relieved that Philip Williams had agreed to become the College Dean. *'All this will add to the charm and attraction'* of the post, he wrote. *'There could hardly be a period in the history of the College when the relations between the Dean and the students have ever been more significant. Mind you the mass of the students are solid i.e., they are Chester-like characters who regard the antics as being amusing but not frightfully significant. Anyhow we are all tolerant.'* Chester recalled early summer meeting in Paris with academics at Sciences Po, who had not predicted the ensuing events in the streets of the French capital and around the Sorbonne, Nanterre University in the suburbs, and the Odéon theatre, where the flag of anarchism flew from the roof. *'There was not a hint that the barricades would be shortly up after we left. I suspect we will have quite a bit of trouble in Oxford in the next fortnight but then comes the Long Vacation and who knows what change may occur between the end of June and October. One thing is quite certain – if anything happens in Oxford, however slight, it will be very fully reported by the press.'*

The events of 1968 and beyond certainly made an impact inside the College. Peter Sinclair writes that *'almost half the College's students joined the Tricontinental Revolutionary Movement (TRM). This was 'a broad coalition of Marxists'.'* They organised agitations not only inside the University but also in schools across Oxford. As Dean, Philip Williams collected a number of leaflets they produced for circulation. One set out an agenda for militant action, designed to democratise the schools by sweeping away examinations, hierarchies, discipline and other symbols of bourgeois oppression. Its aim was to attract boys and girls into the College for training in the revolutionary cause, through holding a workshop or teach in. But that particular leaflet drew some perhaps unconscious attention to Nuffield's famed empiricism and realism. It promised the children there would be a disco held to round off the evening after their rigorous training session. And Sinclair notes – as had Chester – that Students in the College who *'thought parliamentary democracy was not altogether yet ready for the plughole of history, and from the Labour left rightwards formed a quite separate group. Three Nuffield Students maintained particularly warm personal relationships across that divide. All were economists – Andrew Glyn, Athar Hussain and Nick Stern'.*

But others on the left in the College who were not student revolutionaries were also critical of Nuffield's dominant ethos during the Chester years. Alan Fox, as Research Fellow in industrial sociology was particularly dismissive of the role of the College as the academic arm of the Establishment of the 'great and the good'. As he wrote in his unpublished autobiography: '*Sometimes they came for discussion and advice; sometimes we needed something from them; sometimes there was a concern by College Fellows to disseminate among the relevant sections of the Establishment certain ideas for action upon some important public issue. For any one or more of these reasons it might be considered desirable as a way of winning friends, influencing people and creating obligations, to invite them for a weekend of wining and dining in the very comfortable College surroundings. There, after some good High Table food, amply reinforced from a well stocked wine cellar they were apt to become more confiding, more expansive, more receptive of sagacious advice, and if necessary cunningly constructed argument. Other weapons were not neglected. 'When in doubt', said one of the College's most prestigious Fellows in a talk given every year to the new intake of research graduates 'caress their egos'. This was actually a well known aphorism from Margery Perham on how colonial governors should be interviewed.*

Fox disliked the competitive, assertive atmosphere in the College during his time there. 'To show hesitancy, tentativeness, lack of self confidence was fatal', he recalled.' The dominant if unspoken ethos was – if you don't have it in the shop window you don't have it.' He believed this attitude was a reflection of the modern academic who could not be said to have arrived professionally until he had gone public. 'I do not mean by this merely the publication of one's work in specialist monographs and learned journals. 'Going public' in the modern world means appearing on television, giving talks on the wireless, advising government departments, sitting on well publicised royal commissions and commissions of inquiry and writing articles and reviews in the up market national press'.

Fox recalled the special significance of the weekly General Seminar that was held in the College in his time where a research student expounded on his research and then submitted himself to critical comment and questioning from his peers and Fellows with Warden Chester normally in the chair. '*All students knew they were on trial*', confessed Fox. '*Warden and Fellows were the all-important confidential referees who would be approached by university authorities when students came to apply for academic jobs. They would be noting not only the performance of the Student delivering the paper but also that of his peers. Who was asking the searching questions with confidence and vigour? Who on the other hand was sitting quiet and mouse-like in the far corner? The nervous tension was almost palpable.'*

Fox was less awe struck than Atticus on the *Sunday Times* with the rituals of High Table. He wrote of the uncongenial environment that the twice-a-week guest night dinners generated for him. *'Of VIP guests, claret and burgundy glowing in the glasses, white jacketed waiters, quiet and deferential, serving at one's left elbow. The withdrawal afterwards to the Green Room with its wall lights soon dispensed in favour of candles in silver candelabra on the long table. The fruit and the nuts, the coffee and talk afterwards in the Senior Common Room...As the bottles emptied and the room became hotter, the sheer clamour made by two or three knowledgeable and highly individual egos, all determined to hold their own in conversation with their neighbours became considerable and of course ever greater since it obliged everybody present to raise their voice still higher in the struggle to compete. A carrying voice was necessary for survival and anybody who could lip read enjoyed a great advantage.'*

But the College was always far more than glitz and glamour. It was highly industrious. The 'golden age' of Chester witnessed an impressive outpouring of published work from the College. The most striking output came interestingly enough from the despised historians. Robert Skidelsky, Student and then Research Fellow, wrote a provocative and highly readable history of the second Labour government that enjoyed widespread public attention on its publication around the time of the 1967 devaluation. Skidelsky went on to write a more controversial and overly sympathetic biography of Sir Oswald Mosley. On one occasion in the summer of 1968, he dined the old Fascist and his wife Diana in the College Senior Common Room. Perhaps it was just a coincidence that it was on the same evening the University's West Indian Society held a disco in the Junior Common Room below. Skidelsky's *magnum opus* was to be his magisterial three-volume biography of John Maynard Keynes. His wide interest in international politics and economics coupled with a rather erratic party political odyssey culminated in his elevation to the cross benches of the House of Lords.

Jose Harris, Research Fellow in 1967 and later Fellow of St Catherine's College, came to Nuffield where she completed a study of unemployment policy in Edwardian England and went on to write an authoritative biography of Sir William Beveridge. Brian Harrison was another diligent Fellow in history. He came to Nuffield to complete his doctoral thesis on the drink trade in the Victorian Age. A formidably well-organised scholar with a huge and intimidating filing system, Harrison used to hold informal and stimulating seminars in his book-lined room in College on topical issues of historical controversy, in particular on Edward Thompson's *Making of the English Working Class*. A Fellow of Corpus Christi College, he was editor of the *New Oxford Dictionary of National Biography* after the tragic death of Colin Matthew. Harrison has just completed a two-volume history of Britain since 1951 for Oxford University Press. Another influential historian who began his researches at the College was Gareth Stedman-Jones, whose doctoral thesis, on outcast London at the end of the nineteenth century. Paul Addison's *Road to 1945* still remains a classic account of British domestic politics in wartime. He is also the author of other studies of the 1940s and two sympathetic and readable volumes on Winston Churchill. Another Student was Patricia Hollis, a Labour peer, who was a prominent academic at the University of East Anglia. She wrote an unsparing biography of Jennie Lee, Nye Bevan's wife, that revealed her idiosyncracies as well as the importance of her life in the Labour Movement.

The high quality of modern history output from Nuffield may have come as something of an embarrassment to Warden Chester. But after all, he was also a historian. He wrote a massive, officially commissioned volume on the nationalised industries as well as a useful book on the history of the social sciences in Oxford. He had planned to write a history of the College but this was not completed before his death.

The 'golden age' was already beginning to fade, during the final years of the Chester era. The most unpleasant unexpected event came with the College's financial mini crisis that broke in 1973, as a plunging stock market after the Yom Kippur War in the Middle East brought turbulence to the global economic system and quadrupled oil prices.

Nuffield was forced to introduce an emergency austerity programme which involved a necessary cut of nearly a third in its total current expenditure over the next four years. As a result, the College under Chester was required reluctantly to restrain its affluent lifestyle. This did not prove to be as drastic as it had once been feared and, with prudent management, Nuffield soon began to restore its previously sound financial position. But the events of the mid 1970s came as a warning that the College's prosperity could not be taken for granted. A number of changes were made that lessened the relative comfort for the Fellows and Students. Waiter service for all meals in Hall ended except on High Table nights. The cleaning and maintenance grew less intensive. Students were compelled to make their own beds. Fellows were forced to share secretaries. It could hardly be described as the arrival of a new Age of Austerity. However, as the only resident Fellow, Philip Williams insisted in having written into the College record that once the financial crisis was over the retrenchment measures would be withdrawn and life at Nuffield would return to what it had been before. This did not happen.

Warden Chester's Valedictory Address

On the eve of his retirement in August 1978, Norman Chester made his own assessment of where the College stood after his twenty-four years as Warden;

> 'Though young in years and small in size it has already established an international reputation in the social sciences. It has attracted a distinguished group of Fellows who are widely known not only in the academic world but also in the world of practical affairs. Its Students now occupy the majority of Economics and Politics fellowships in other Oxford colleges, hold Professorships in a dozen or so countries and are already to be found in many important public and political positions. Yet Nuffield is almost the smallest Oxford College and far smaller than most of the University departments of Economics and Social Studies with which it competes. It has achieved its status by a

policy of elitism ... The College was established for a purpose more specific than to be a place of learning or a home for post-graduates. These objectives were subsumed under a main purpose – the study of social, economic and political problems. The emphasis was on research rather than teaching. In a small institution comparatively small shifts of emphasis may, over a period, change the main course of its contribution. Only by returning from time to time to the main purpose can the institution be kept on course'.

In his valedictory address to the College's Governing Body, which he made a month later, Chester gave eloquent voice to his own concept of Nuffield and what he saw as its current and future problems. He continued to believe that the College should be true to what he saw as the wishes of its Founder – *'to be of direct help to the sufferings and problems of humanity'*. Moreover, Chester took a rather exalted view of the role of academics at a time when their status and well-being were coming under real threat. *'Academics on the whole lead a pleasant life. We may not be paid as much as the higher bureaucracy and management. But we are academics because that is what we wanted to be. We can pursue the studies which interest us the most and work at our own pace. We carry a good deal of public esteem. We may, therefore, come to believe that whatever way we spend our time is inevitably of value precisely because we are university teachers. I have never thought that being a don was an end in itself, an uncontestable reason for living. To be a don whose teaching and research may make some contribution to the solution or alleviation of current social, economic and political problems has always seemed to me to give the best of both possible worlds – the reflective and the practical'.*

Chester went so far as to suggest that the presence of Students in the College put Nuffield in the same category and with the same broad purpose as other Oxford colleges such as Wolfson and Linacre, and that the College would be regarded like St Antony's as a home for post graduates. This posed a danger that Fellows would be elected for their teaching abilities and not to increase the College's capacity to study social and economic problems.

The retiring Warden was also troubled by what he saw as the relentless growth of B Phil students in the college, particularly in economics. But this was perhaps inevitable with the growing professionalism of the subject with its increasing emphasis on mathematics and econometrics. *'Even those who have spent three years on the economics tripos at Cambridge or who have done the majority of papers in PPE in economics feel inadequate to face the world without two more years largely of economic theory'*, Chester admitted. As a result the College had to devote more of its resources to meet those new needs. Ideally he would have preferred post B Phil students to come to the College in order to prepare a doctoral thesis. But as Chester confessed; *'The fact must be faced. The economics side of the college attracts some of our ablest students. We devote a good deal of our time and resources in perfecting their training as professional economists and then the bulk of them disappear to the World Bank, merchant banks and to teaching. Very few indeed are available to increase the capacity of the College to undertake research into economic problems'*.

Chester's valedictory address to the College included an attack on what he described as the *'seduction of history'*. He suggested that history graduates from Oxford were more able than those graduating in PPE and that the College prize research fellowships came mostly from history with the smallest number from economics. Perhaps more seriously he recognised that the College could not attract able research fellows in 'subjects of interest to industry'. In this, Nuffield reflected a pattern found in the rest of Oxford and in other British universities.

Chester went on to lament what he regarded as the relative failure in the College to promote fruitful co-operation between academics and non-academics, as had been envisaged by the Founder and Lindsay and then exemplified in Nuffield's wartime private conferences. It was true that men and women from the world outside Nuffield still came to dinner on Wednesday and Friday nights. The Gwilym Gibbon fellowships and the media fellowships were important in establishing important personal connections outside academia. Some Visiting Fellows – notably Shirley Williams, Samuel Brittan, and Douglas Hurd – took a keen interest in the affairs of the College. A few specialist conferences – on the Donovan Commission, on Redcliffe-Maud's commission on local government and the treatment of the political parties by the BBC – had taken place during his time as Warden but these were usually ad hoc and one-off occasions with no follow up. Sadly there was no attempt to resume the private conference idea that had been relatively successful during the war years. Despite this, Chester doubted whether there was *'any other small group of academics'* who enjoyed *'so many close contacts with the various worlds of practical affairs'*. They were still able to move around the corridors of Westminster and Whitehall and local government and trade unions with great ease. *'They are even not unknown in banking and the City'*, he noted. But the Warden also recognised that the fewest contacts made by the College during the 1970s were those with business and industry, something that had not been the case before the 1960s.

The Warden also used the opportunity in his 1978 farewell address to discuss what he believed went to the very heart of Nuffield's traditionally-declared purpose as a problem solver of contemporary issues. Nuffield had wanted to encourage academics as *'self-motivating, self-directing'* individuals. *'They did not come to the College to join a team or a centre established to further a specific piece of research. The Fellows were encouraged to concentrate on topics that stimulated them'*, he explained. Chester gave the example of Ian Little who as an economist had started his research work with a concentration on welfare economics, and moved on to fiscal policy, and then to investment appraisals in developing countries. The Warden conceded that this meant that at any one time the research and writing going on in the College might *'not conform to the popular criteria of the most pressing economic, social and political problems of the age'*. But Chester also believed that the Nuffield system would be *'working reasonably well'* if over a period of time *'the College's contribution was significant and worthwhile'*. However, he accepted that this was dependent on having a group of Fellows trained in the social sciences who were *'sufficiently moved by social, economic and political problems to wish to devote their time and intellect to their study'*.

Chester always opposed institutional approaches to social research. He did not regard eminent independent bodies such as the National Institute of Economic and Social Research or PEP, later the Policy Studies Institute, as satisfactory models because their programmes implied that those who undertook research were of less significance than the subject that was chosen. Such an attitude stemmed in part from his personal experiences in Whitehall during the war. As Chester observed, he had been involved in trying to identify areas in urgent need of research and had found it *'seldom a rewarding exercise'*.

> *'In any case such a large number of potential subjects was usually located that the subsequent choice of priorities was largely dictated by current fashions. Most important, in the end, whether any satisfactory results were achieved depended on whether sufficiently able people were not merely available but were excited by the prospect of undertaking the project'.*

Chester did not deny there were all kinds and levels of research staff tackling one project after another. But he also believed that such institutions attracted or retained the most able people in their field because such people did not like working in a hierarchical system but preferred to make their own decisions.

Chester was particularly irritated at his leaving occasion by a public broadside he had just received from Bernard Donoughue, a former College Student who in 1974 moved from the LSE's department of government to become chief policy adviser to the Wilson and then the Callaghan governments. Donoughue had complained to the Warden that nothing written by anybody in the College over the previous four to five years had 'helped' the government and that as a result Nuffield was failing to fulfil the original purposes for which it had been established. In fact, it had just become yet another academic institution with no distinctive attributes of its own. Donoughue had always argued that Nuffield should have developed a Kennedy style school of government on the Harvard University model.

In his angry response to this charge of irrelevance, Chester, perhaps unconsciously, undermined the whole Lindsay vision of close collaboration and the search for common ground between academia and the world of the public policy makers. He asserted that a mere *'current problem solving academic institution was a will of the wisp'*. Chester went on to argue;

'The time scale is quite different. Governments usually defer recognising a problem until there is little or no time to undertake all the research necessary for the exploration of possible solutions. Moreover problem solving is not just a matter of research or even just the exercise of a trained mind. One has to take an account of the political and administrative possibilities. Such considerations do not come readily to the academic working in the University. They are ingredients which probably only those close to ministers and Whitehall contribute'. Chester argued that *'the great bulk of the work involved in the decision making process in government could only effectively be undertaken inside Whitehall. One can bring in outside academics, one can commission particular pieces of research to be undertaken outside but no government yet has found their policy decisions made for them by purely academic activity'.*

Donoughue, in a lecture he gave to the College in 1987, confessed that Nuffield still meant a great deal to him and that it remained special because of its close involvement with public policy-makers and that this was one of the notable features of the Chester years. He urged the College *'to keep one foot in the impure world of prickly politicians and soiled stockbrokers and merchant bankers'* and never become *'just another academic monastic haven of pure econometricians or pure political theorists unskilled by trade or matters of state'.* It was a friendly warning, but reflected genuine concern that Nuffield's 'golden age' was passing into history and its future direction in the post-Chester years looked uncertain.

However, memories of Chester's time as Warden do not deserve to end on a sour or questioning note. Peter Sinclair remembers his own time at Nuffield with nostalgia, but in doing so, his words are echoed by many other Students who passed through the College during its 'golden age' of Norman Chester. *'The College was firmly administered, perhaps over-administered. But we were all fond of Norman Chester despite his idiosyncrasies and distaste for history and for abstract ideas because we really knew he had his Students' welfare at heart. All of us, economists and non-economists saw how privileged we were; we discussed everything under the sun. It was a wonderful place to serve such a special academic apprenticeship. And the beauty is it still is, just that.'*

A New Nuffield for New Times:
The Search for a Role

The end of man is an action and not a thought, though it were the noblest.

Thomas Carlyle in *Sartor Resartus*, quoted by
Nevil Johnson in his retirement speech 5 July 1996.

The Wardens in Turbulent Times

The College survived and advanced through an often difficult period of uncertainty and turbulence in the outside world during the thirty years that followed Norman Chester's retirement. The four Wardens who succeeded him faced a much harsher public policy climate than he had ever experienced, as the social sciences in Britain came under sustained ideological attack from a Conservative government led by Margaret Thatcher. The return of mass unemployment in the early 1980s, the cuts in public spending in education and apparent threats to the welfare state indicated that the era of the post-war social settlement in which the College had thrived was well and truly over. The worsening financial stringency added to the gloom, as new posts in Britain's universities, especially in the social sciences, declined and Nuffield Students could no longer assume they were heading for a secure future as life-long academics in a university of their choice after leaving the College.

The 'middle way' or social democratic nature of the College made it uneasily placed to come to terms with the more bracing climate of the 1980s. Few Fellows were actually sympathetic to the politics of Margaret Thatcher. Suggestions that the new Prime Minister should be considered as a Visiting Fellow did not get far. Publicly she seemed hostile, or at best indifferent, to the importance of the social sciences in public policy-making, if their findings were contrary to her own instincts and intuition. Moreover, as some of the main academic interests at Nuffield were focused on controversial questions such as social mobility, class, income and wealth distribution, it was unlikely that Conservative governments would take much notice of their research findings if they conflicted with their own public policy preferences.

The social sciences were coming under critical scrutiny. The government even established an inquiry, chaired by Lord Rothschild, on whether it might be sensible to abolish the Social Science Research Council. While the subsequent report gave that organisation a reprieve, the word 'Science' was dropped from its title and it became the Economics and Social Research Council (ESRC). The Warwick University Industrial Relations Research Unit also came under serious threat of closure and it was the subject of a specific government-backed investigation. Again, the Unit fended off the dangers with high professionalism. Of course, Nuffield was not so dependent on state funding for its very existence to be under any direct challenge, but the College could not ignore the less than enthusiastic official attitude to the social sciences in general in its own activities.

It was, however, always a caricature to suggest that sociology and the other allied social sciences were unrepentantly left wing whatever academic figures like former Nuffield Fellow Max Beloff at All Souls might have claimed. At no stage, not even during the later years of Norman Chester, did the College recruit Fellows who could remotely be described as Marxist. There seemed to be little enthusiasm at the prospect of any well-known left-wing academic coming to Nuffield. This became most palpable in the case of Claus Offe. The renowned Frankfurt sociologist was turned down for a Fellowship at Nuffield. Anthony Heath was seen, by a narrow margin, as a better bet. In fact, the College's traditional emphasis on empiricism, pragmatism and positivism continued to remain paramount. But this did not mean more of the same. It would be an exaggeration to suggest that Nuffield lost an Empire and failed to find a role for itself in the 1980s and 1990s. For the College it was not really an age of stagnation. On the contrary, often without any grandiose pronouncements, Nuffield was moving perceptibly in new directions and away from its past image during those years. Chelly Halsey once described Nuffield under Chester as a 'Mancunian institution'. Now he suggested the College was growing 'more ecumenical'.

The internationalisation of the College in its academic achievements represented a recurring and impressive trend after 1979. If the world of 'official' Britain could turn its face against Nuffield and the social sciences, this was certainly not true of other countries. The College's academic reputation in economics and sociology, as we shall see, grew impressively during the thirty years that followed Chester's retirement.

The Wardens of the period (Michael Brock, David Cox, Tony Atkinson and now Steve Nickell) were quite different from one another in their styles and in their views on how the College should develop in the future, but all of them reflected the growing uncertainties of the age. For the most part, they did not regard themselves as visionaries but essentially consolidators and administrators who were deeply conscious of Chester's enduring legacy. What they found difficult to do, as John Darwin explains, was *'to resolve the unavoidable tensions'* that existed in Nuffield between the original ideals of the College, and the fact that the Fellows had to win and maintain their intellectual prestige in a wider academic world that was increasingly unfriendly to the kind of ideals that Lindsay had evoked in the 1930. The educational authorities now demanded evidence of academic performance through refereed output under the treadmill of the Research Assessment Exercise.

Michael Brock, the Warden from 1978 to 1987, might look at first sight a rather surprising appointment. A quintessentially Oxford political historian with a recently published volume on the 1832 Reform Act, he could hardly be described as a social scientist or a scholar of 'modern' studies. In fact, Brock was only elected as Warden after a stiff contest, when he narrowly defeated the LSE sociologist Ernest Gellner and Chelly Halsey and Aubrey Silberston, who were the internal candidates, to succeed Chester. Brock's administrative skills had been well proven under Sir Isaiah Berlin's presidency of Wolfson College, and he possessed expertise on the intricacies of Oxford University politics. Both were, perhaps, the deciding factors in his election. Some dismayed College Fellows regarded Brock's victory as a triumph for what they saw as the old guard in Nuffield and a backward step for the College's role as a graduate centre for the social sciences.

However, the politics Fellow Nevil Johnson was one who pointed to clear signs of change after Brock's arrival. *'Very soon one noticed that the Governing Body was more often confronted with issues and problems imposed upon it by outside circumstances – in the University, in the funding agencies, and in the sphere of government and politics. Moreover none of them could be resolved by the College alone.'* Johnson saw a clear change in style in the Warden's conduct of College business. *'Leaving on one side Michael Brock's manic scribbling in blue and red on his copy of the Governing Body agenda, the minutes were punctuated more and more by terse headings and there was a shift towards a more purely businesslike style in the recording of discussions and conclusions.'* Perhaps it was inevitable that Brock's period as Warden necessitated something of a holding operation.

Brock admitted as much in his 1988 valedictory address when he highlighted what he saw as his accomplishments. It is true that he insisted the College's *'troubles in the past'* with the University's Hebdomadal Council now *'belonged to a different era'*. Moreover, he believed there were no longer those in the University *'who did not acknowledge the central importance of social studies'*. But Brock was well aware that in Oxford *'the undergraduate honours work commanded the big battalions'* and as things grew tighter such numerical preponderance might be used by the other Oxford Colleges against Nuffield with *'dangerous effect'*.

However, the outgoing Warden admitted he was worried about where the College was going academically. His most outspoken remarks concerned what he believed to be the inability of the social scientists to communicate the results of their work to the wider world.

> *'At some stage almost every Fellow in Nuffield ought to command an audience which goes beyond the academic grove ... What is discovered here about social mobility, regional patterns of unemployment, the effect of house price movements, methods of privatisation and about many other problems ought to be known by the people who are in a position to affect policies and events'.*

Brock, however, was keen to reassure his audience that such remarks did not mean that he was intrinsically hostile to the use of theory. As he ruminated:

'The great changes come, not so much through the influencing of today's policies as through shifts effected over long periods of time in the climate of opinion.'

David Cox, a quietly spoken and rather self-effacing man, was one of the country's leading statisticians when he was elected as Warden in succession to Brock. Cox had spent the previous twenty years of his distinguished academic life as a professor of statistics at Imperial College, University of London. Cox impressed many Nuffield Fellows at his interview for the Wardenship by his declared intention to raise Nuffield's academic social science reputation internationally. He admitted in 2007 that he had been in *'total'* ignorance of Oxford University before his arrival at Nuffield and that he had known very little about the College either. However, to the delight of Nuffield's quantitative sociologists, most notably John Goldthorpe, Cox gave his enthusiastic and active support to a more data-driven, statistical approach to the social sciences in what was to become an intensification of a growing tendency inside the College. *'Before he became the Warden you felt that your work in sociology was going against the tide in the College'*, argues Goldthorpe. *'Cox gave us terrific encouragement. He was easily accessible and helpful. At last we belonged.'*

It was under Cox that the College began to establish much closer links with other centres of learning in the social sciences outside Britain. In Goldthorpe's opinion this was the key to propelling Nuffield into the mainstream of European sociology. It was a priority that succeeded. The fact that it was a college in Oxford that had become the focus for a particular kind of sociology was not the point. The work that Goldthorpe and his fellow sociologists in the College were doing could have been done anywhere. With Cox's enthusiastic backing, Nuffield began to reach out more assertively to the wider world of the social sciences in continental Europe and the United States.

Cox seemed less focused than either Chester or Brock had been on furthering the College's standing in an always suspicious, and still often resentful, University. He was less keen on the intricacies of Hebdomadal Council politics. As a result, Nuffield was perceived by some Fellows to grow at least a little semi-detached and inward-looking from any direct Oxford concerns during the Cox years. There was certainly no wish to take up Brock's valedictory admonition to ensure there were more historians around the College. Under Cox the three Groups – economics, politics and sociology – grew more formalised. As a result they were able to determine who joined them and what they were doing. Unfortunately there was no longer room in Nuffield for many whose research interests failed to fit into the rigidities of those three self-defined categories of social science. Cox's expertise in statistics was much used by Ray Fitzpatrick (Professor of Public Health and Primary Care) and Lucy Carpenter (Reader in Statistical Epidemiology) who came in 1996.

Cox was also concerned to place Nuffield's domestic administration in the capable hands of professional managers. In this, he followed what was then becoming a recognisable trend across much of British higher education, as the status and authority of administrators grew more apparent at the expense of the academics. The days of seconding existing Nuffield Fellows to be Domestic Bursars were apparently coming to an end. Simon Porter's appointment was the first of its kind in the Bursary, and in Goldthorpe's words he proved to be *'efficient but unobtrusive'* in his work. There was not much apparent resistance to this decision among the Fellows. Perhaps many of them acknowledged that the change at least provided them with the opportunity to concentrate more exclusively on their own researches. In 1996 Porter was succeeded by Gwilym Hughes. However, this was always to be a matter of balance. Handing over administrative authority and power to non-academics may have ensured greater efficiency in the conduct of College business, but it was sometimes unclear where the ultimate decision-making authority lay on domestic matters. Cox liked to work through sub-committees and issues raised and discussed at Governing Body level were in effect decided upon before they reached its agenda. It is also worth pointing out that the College's highly successful investment policy remained firmly in the capable hands of Nuffield Fellows – most notably those of Christopher Bliss and Laurence Whitehead.

Tony Atkinson was elected Warden in 1994 and remained in that post for over ten years until 2005. He was the first academic economist to run Nuffield. His research interests were mainly focused on poverty and income distribution and social welfare issues, increasingly in a European context. Atkinson continues to examine the economic implications of the reform of the welfare state. He came to the College after a distinguished career at the University of Essex and then as a professor of political economy and Fellow of Churchill College, Cambridge. Atkinson remains a prolific and diligent writer. He even continued with his researches while at Nuffield where he was granted the first sabbatical leave that had ever been given to the College Warden. During his nine month's absence he worked on a long-term project with the construction of long-run estimates of the distribution of income in OECD countries and the explanation of the long-run evolution of inequality. But like Cox, Atkinson did not bring any Grand Design to the running of Nuffield. Nor did he launch any dramatic strategic initiatives. But he did believe that as Warden his important purpose was to defend the College against its critics and he did so with some success. Atkinson claimed in his final report to Nuffield in 2005 that the College's very *'survival'* during his time as Warden had been in itself an achievement. But he also recognised that the College would need to raise its waning public profile again in the future. *'It is a remarkable institution but it is not as well known as it ought to be, either inside or outside Oxford'*, Atkinson pointed out. He admitted to his colleagues that much of his time as Warden had been spent in trying to explain that Nuffield was *'not like other Colleges'*. Atkinson argued that it had become *'in some respects ... an inter-disciplinary University department'*. *'Not only does the College not fit neatly into the University organisation chart, but also in substantial terms the new Departments have increasingly taken over a number of roles of the College in the fields of graduate teaching and research.'* In future, Atkinson thought this development of separate departments for politics, economics and sociology would require Nuffield *'to rethink its interstitial position'* in the University. It needed to consider how it was going to complement the new departments, for example with *'a greater emphasis on interdisciplinarity and the College's relations outside the social sciences, for example with history and statistics'.* But would such a development be possible without energetic leadership in the College and perhaps against the vested interests that were growing in the three newly created departments, even if two of them were run by Nuffield Fellows? Atkinson believed it would be a mistake to try and enforce interdisciplinary development on unwilling researchers. An emphasis on interdisciplinarity could *'not be imposed from above but most come from below'*, he accepted. Atkinson argued that such a trend would require *'people who were well grounded in their own disciplines to want to collaborate on a problem where their skills are complementary'.*

Nuffield's Core Goes International

All three core social science subjects at Nuffield experienced considerable change during the Brock, Cox and Atkinson years as they grew more international in their interests.

It was always rather an oversimplification to suggest that any of the Nuffield economists before 1979 were pure Keynesians. Indeed, it is questionable whether such economists ever really existed. Even Keynes said he was not one himself. But on the other hand, the College's economic Fellows had neither advocated nor predicted the rise of what became known as neo-Liberalism after the 1980s, with its commitment to deregulation, privatisation, firm control of the money supply and curbs on trade union power in an increasingly open market economy. Two of them signed the famous open letter from 364 of the country's leading academic economists, criticising the Chancellor Geoffrey Howe's 1981 Budget as likely to worsen the economic outlook with a predicated substantial rise in unemployment, which did indeed happen. But most, if not all, of the College economics Fellows were engaged in mathematical economics, game theory and abstract model building. This was the growing trend in academic economics internationally and Nuffield remained very much at its cutting edge, both in its recruitment and in the publications that emerged from the College from the economists. While there was some interest shown in the trend to greater specialisation and theoretical sophistication in Whitehall, most Nuffield economists were no longer travelling up to London on the 8.55 train to seconded jobs in government departments. However, the College's ties with the Bank of England and to a lesser extent the City of London have perhaps grown closer than they had been in the post-Chester years. Mervyn King, the current Bank of England Governor, is now a Visiting Fellow at Nuffield.

The actual academic quality of the Nuffield economists probably grew much higher in the 1980s and beyond. One of the most eminent of the new generation of economists at the College is David Hendry. His work, especially in economic forecasting and econometric modelling, is highly regarded internationally.

Nor were all the College economists unconnected with the public policy world. Paul Klemperer, Professorial Fellow since 1995, was a member of the Stern review into climate change and the Gowers review of intellectual property rights. He was also a member of the Competition Commission for a number of years. *'It would be hard to imagine a scholar who combines more harmoniously high theory and the practical implementation of good policies'*, says Christopher Bliss. Klemperer was also a government advisor and collaborator in the design of the 2000 Spectrum Auction of UK mobile phone lines which raised £21.5 billion and this, according to Bliss, was far more successful than several parallel exercises on the European continent. Klemperer's main research interests lie in industrial economics, competition policy and auction design. Some of his work was done in conjunction with his wife, Meg Meyer, a specialist in economic theories about reputation and careers who in 1988 became only the third woman to be elected an Official Fellow.

John Muellbauer was elected to an Official Fellowship in 1980. He is best known internationally for his work on consumption theory. In recent years he has written extensively on the British housing market both in journals and newspapers. More recently his research interests have also included macroeconomic modelling and a study of the South

African economy. Kevin Roberts, a former Student and a Professorial Fellow since 1999, has specialised in welfare and public economics.

Another important economics Fellow in the College is Neil Shephard. In September 2007 he was made research director of the Oxford-Man Institute of Quantitative Finance, which claims to be the world's leading centre for quantitative finance. The newly founded body is funded by the Man Group, one of the world's largest hedge fund providers.

In politics the historical bias in the College grew more pronounced from the 1980s onwards. David Butler, with his interest in the realities of contemporary British politics, found himself in an increasingly isolated position, particularly after the death of Philip Williams. There were some obvious signs that the subject in Nuffield was moving towards a more sophisticated mathematical approach in the use of electoral data, indicated by the flow of authoritative books and articles on British general elections and voting behaviour abroad written by Anthony Heath, Clive Payne and Geoff Evans,. There has been a clear convergence with the sociologists in the College over recent years.

But this was never to be the whole picture of what has happening to the study of politics in Nuffield. A number of Fellows believed in the academic importance of comparative studies. These included, most notably, Laurence Whitehead on Latin America, Vincent Wright and Jeremy Richardson on Europe, and Byron Shafer on the United States. Most of them were well aware of the latest forms of methodology originating from American political science and they used those techniques when they deemed it was necessary. However, their research was not completely closed off from an engagement with the outside world. Nor was it contemptuous of history.

Whitehead was particularly successful in building up fruitful academic networks between the College and overseas institutions, especially in Latin America and East Asia. His main focus was on a comparative study of democratisation. Whitehead was also concerned with the concept of citizen security. His most important published work, *Democratization: Theory and Experience*, was published in 2002.

Another Fellow in the College who combined academic research with non-academic action was Iain McLean, who succeeded David Butler as an Official Fellow in politics in 1992. He is now regarded as something of a polymath whose broad academic interests would have pleased Lindsay and Chester. Once a political historian and biographer of Keir Hardie and author of *The Legend of Red Clydeside*, McLean stretched his expertise to cover rational choice theory, model building and other modern approaches to political science and he was willing to take risks in the breadth of his expertise. McLean also wrote a short volume on Adam Smith (complete with a preface from the Prime Minister Gordon Brown). He is now the director of the Public Policy Unit in the University's politics and international relations department. McLean coordinates a team of mainly young academic technocrats and functionaries, some of whom are or were employed in the 10 Downing Street Policy Unit like David Halpern and Stewart Wood, in what is called the Options for Britain project. This follows on from a similar exercise that was carried out eleven years ago which also had a strong Nuffield input. The current project is partly funded by the charitable Gatsby Foundation of Lord Sainsbury (once a Visiting Fellow and now an Honorary Fellow of the College) as well as by the ESRC. It is more than just a think-tank for New Labour. Conservatives as well as Liberal Democrats are also involved in the project. It certainly reflects a welcome shift in emphasis to a more policy-oriented political science emerging from the College.

Sociology grew to be a more dominant academic force in the College from the 1980s. While it was never to achieve an undisputed intellectual hegemony it did make important advances into both Nuffield's politics and economics groups. And it was a particular strain of sociology that flourished in consistent line with Nuffield's original bias towards quantitative, data-driven social research. Its main focus was concentrated on social mobility and electoral behaviour. Theories based on the 'relics' of historical knowledge or understanding of the pioneering theorists of sociology, Weber, Mannheim and Pareto, were regarded as less relevant for understanding the complexities of the modern world.

A number of recently-elected Fellows have reinforced the quantitative tendencies of Nuffield sociology. These include Colin Mills from the LSE as well as Peter Hedström and Nan Dirk de Graaf. All of them have been influenced by the work of John Goldthorpe whose analysis of social mobility has won him and the College international renown in sociology. Goldthorpe has continued his researches in his retirement. His work has been recognised, particularly in Sweden.

But again, this is not the whole of the Nuffield story in sociology as the important work of the industrial sociologist Duncan Gallie and an Official Fellow from 1985 indicates. He was the main director of the ESRC's first funded employment at work programme which was carried out during the 1990s. The resulting volume that was published in 1998 challenged much of the conventional wisdom about the British labour market of the time and although the programme's recommendations did not make any noticeable impact on the government's public policy, its findings raised serious questions and provided a rich amount of empirical data evidence for a more radical approach to employment strategy based on those increasingly forgotten ethical values of equality and social justice. It is a pity those concepts became increasingly unfashionable and of no direct concern to governments during the 1990s. Gallie's impressive work on what has also been happening in wider European labour markets drew necessary attention to what have become relatively neglected areas of policy thinking; namely the quality of working life, the inadequacy of Britain's productivity performance and its persistently poor record of technical education in remedying chronic skilled labour shortages. Here again was a good example of how applied social science research could become of urgent relevance to the world of the public policy-makers. The fact that governments in Britain chose to ignore Gallie's important findings does not make them any the less vital both in theory and practice. In his work he was following very much in the Lindsay/Chester tradition.

Gordon Marshall (a Student from 1974 to 1977) was another influential sociologist at Nuffield. He was an Official Fellow at the College from 1993 until 1999. Since 2003 he has been the Vice-

Chancellor of Reading University but was also chief executive and deputy chairman of the ESRC from 2000 to 2002. Marshall spent an earlier period of his academic life as a Postdoctoral Research Fellow at Nuffield, followed by academic posts at Essex University from 1978 to 1990 and then briefly at the University of Bath.

Marshall's initial focus research was on Max Weber and the origins of capitalism. His first book, based on his doctoral thesis supervised by John Goldthorpe, concerned Presbyterianism and Calvinism in seventeenth-century Scotland. But later he immersed himself in the complexities of social mobility and class. In his co-authored volume, *Against The Odds? Social Class and Social Justice in Industrial Societies*, published in 1997, Marshall and his colleagues took a cautious and nuanced view of the relationship between social class, social mobility and social justice through educational opportunities. Their research was rooted, in Nuffield style, in a range of social survey empirical data.

What was clear from earlier work by Marshall and others, published in a co-authored volume (*Social Class in Modern Britain*), was a rejection of either a liberal individualistic view of upward social mobility or any Marxist conception of class. Marshall saw social change as not being *'the result of some underlying logic or dialectic in the development of industrial-capitalist societies'*. He indicated that neither he nor his co-authors gave support for *'historicists of right or left in their analysis of demographic and social-political class formation'*.

His single authored volume, *Repositioning Class: Social Inequality in Industrial Societies*, published in 1997, brought together a number of his essays from the previous decade, in which he argues that public pronouncements about the death of social class were greatly exaggerated. As Marshall wrote in the preface to his 1997 volume, *'Social class is as important to the understanding of late twentieth-century industrial societies as it was to their early capitalist counterparts and class analysis is probably now in a healthier state than at any previous time in its long sociological history'*.

Marshall added that his approach was guided in its methodological principles by *'a suspicion of grand theory, a preference for theories of the middle range, hostility to historicism of the political left and right alike and the attempt to match testable (middle range) propositions to appropriate empirical data'*. In saying this, Marshall articulated what were always the basic core beliefs of the Nuffield 'school' of sociology.

It was his connection of concepts of social justice with social mobility that Marshall made a personal contribution. He argued persuasively that political intervention is required to prevent class inequalities from impeding the advance of social justice. Marshall suggested that *'if children from advantaged backgrounds suffered educational failure, their class position made it likely they would be able to call upon other resources, perhaps most importantly in the form of class related social networks, which can protect them from the consequences'*.

During the 1990s Marshall also played an important part in the creation of the department of sociology at Oxford University in the teeth of some stiff resistance, especially from among the political scientists who wanted to subsume the subject under their discipline. Marshall's undoubted abilities as an administrator led to his promotion to the post of chief executive of the ESRC. More recently Marshall appears to have cast some doubt on the seriousness of sociology as an academic subject. In his role as Vice-Chancellor of Reading University, he was forced to close down its sociology department as a cost-cutting measure.

For the most part, since the later 1980s the three distinctive Nuffield subject areas of economics, politics and sociology, organised as self-selecting Groups, seemed to grow more rigid; less in touch with one another as individuals or teams, and as a result less collegial. The promise of earlier generations at the College with their broader vision appeared to decline. There was to be no dramatic change or rupture that stemmed from any conscious decision but what happened did reflect a perceptible gradual shift, a tendency rather than a trend. The result was to make Nuffield a less interesting and perhaps less important institution, at least to many non-academics in the outside world.

Nuffield's Critics from Outside and Within

Andrew Adonis, a Student and then a Research Fellow at the College during the 1980s, and now an Education Minister and a member of the House of Lords (after a sustained period in the 10 Downing Street Policy Unit) expresses his real regret that the College has developed what he believes to be *'a distinct institutional disdain for the world of politics and government'*.

Martin Wolf was an economics Student at the College from 1969 to 1971, before he went to work at the World Bank in Washington. Later he was a Visiting Fellow. Wolf is one of the world's leading economic commentators. His perceptive and lucid columns in the pages of the *Financial Times* are required reading for anybody who wants to understand what is happening to global capitalism. Wolf's views about Nuffield are trenchant and cannot easily be dismissed as of no significance. *'A whale beached by time, magnificent but no longer vital'* is how he judges the College today. Wolf points out that the existence of the well-resourced Department of Economics in Oxford University and the creation of Oxonia (the Oxford Institute of Economic Policy) have both helped to marginalise Nuffield in recent years in economics. But it is worth noting that David Hendry has headed the Department of Economics for most of its existence and Nuffield Fellows both founded and continue to run Oxonia. Wolf is also rather surprised, as are others, at the College's failure to make better use of its Visiting Fellows. Wolf says he has only been invited once to speak at the College beyond the events staged around Stated Meetings. He also regrets that Visiting Fellows do not have enough direct contact with the Students. Wolf would like to see a greater encouragement for interdisciplinary research inside Nuffield and more allocation of College resources to be used by the University. But he is now uncertain whether Nuffield can survive in its current form. *'I fear that the idea of a post graduate College dedicated to the social sciences may now be a bit of an anomaly'*.

David Willetts, the Conservative MP, was another recent Visiting Fellow. He follows in the honourable footsteps of a number of senior Conservatives who came to Nuffield over the years as Visiting Fellows –

most notably Reginald Maudling, Edward Heath, Willie Whitelaw Douglas Hurd, David Howell and Graham Mather. Willetts agrees with some of Wolf's criticisms. He found it useful to pick the brains of Emeritus Fellows like John Goldthorpe on the mysteries of social mobility when he comes down to Nuffield. However, he regretted the lack of any systematic contact with the Students. Willetts may be one of the few politicians in Britain who can hold his own in discussions with Nuffield's economists and sociologists. But he thinks it might be a good idea if the College made more effort to contact and engage with the public policy world. He even suggests Nuffield should buy or rent rooms near Parliament and Whitehall so Fellows could give briefings and lectures on their research findings to the public policy-makers.

The College during the 1980s and 1990s was not free from some criticism by its own Fellows at what it was doing. The most outspoken of them is Chelly Halsey. He concedes that by the middle of the 1990s the College still remained *'relatively highly privileged in the national desert of the social sciences'* which had emerged from Thatcherism. But he also found much to dislike about Nuffield at that time. *'Expansionism under prosperity, individualism under Thatcher and social amnesia under Americanisation have combined to undermine traditional practices'*, he lamented. Halsey grumbled that some Americans in the College seemed to regard the Dining Hall as a *'restaurant where you can grab a sandwich'*. *'American and continental senior visitors and too few sponsors are responsible enough to work on the subtle task of integrating newcomers into an unfamiliar culture,'* he added. *'Everyone is 'too busy with their own work. Even the mechanics of conversation are not understood.'* He added that the Junior Common Room and the Hall increasingly resembled *'an airport lounge. It is sad to reflect that affluence pays air fares and reduces the quality of collegiate life by adding to the guests and taking away the hosts'*.

But Halsey in the 1990s also criticised Nuffield's efforts to bring academics and non-academics together through the use of the Visiting Fellows system. In this he seemed to question one of the original purposes of the College. Halsey feared there was a danger that if the links grew too close between the College and government and industry, the definition of what were social science problems would be defined not by the Fellows but by politicians and administrators. While Halsey acknowledged that practical problems deserved academic attention and public service justified what the Universities sought from society, the *'proper development'* of the social sciences required freedom for academics to define contemporary problems within the theoretical terms of their own disciplines. Halsey questioned whether Visiting Fellows could find the time in their busy lives to play an active role in the College. *'The paradox is that though Britain is something like three or four times better off than when Nuffield was founded, leisure for measured exchange has become a more and more scarce commodity.'* Halsey wondered out loud whether a College was any longer a suitable place for the kind of public discourse Lindsay and Lord Nuffield had once envisaged. Perhaps that important conversation was no longer needed – or if it was, it were better done somewhere else.

Halsey argued that the College needed to become *'unequivocally the academic partner'* in its relations with the Visiting Fellows. *'Too often I think we slip into the role of handmaiden to interests and definitions of problems by Whitehall'*, he complained. He instanced the Social Mobility project as a success in making a political impact. However, Halsey did not believe the definition of a social or economic problem should be laid down by politicians or public administrators. He recognised the dangers of academic priorities always coming first. They could not pretend they had *'either the political or administrative skill or responsibility'*. Moreover, there was always an obvious danger that academic expertise might be trivialised as the College provided the *'errand boys, information collators, cooks and waiters in an agreeable provincial hotel at which the 'powers' have assembled for the weekend'*.

At times Halsey seems to have been questioning the very basis of quantitative sociology in the College. He pointed out that they once had a *'firm conception of our inheritance through the books left to us by a rather limited number of exceptionally learned men. In sociology we had the shoulders of Max Weber, Emile Durkheim and Pareto on which to stand'*. But College life was no longer dominated by that particular intellectual inheritance. *'Instead we have developed and go on developing techniques for generating and analysing data sets. The speed of computers and the elaboration of models now dominates'*, ruminated Halsey. *'Recruits are not distinguished as adepts in the discussion of the past masters with an agreed set of books they all know intimately.'* Now he believes the basic model for sociology is science rather than the arts and the resulting educational background is not so much particular schools of thought as the common experience of computer literacy which came from *'endless childhood hours with television and computer games'*. Halsey believes such changes are having an effect on academic careers as it is no longer the learned man and woman who is being sought but *'the person who is quick with quantitative methods'*. He warns this might in the end *'break the academic monopoly over learning'*. In short, Halsey appeared to have begun to question the very concept of a residential research College as appropriate for the new age.

'We are philosophically weak', he complains. The three groups in Nuffield *'do not fit into any coherent definition of a College for the social studies'* and their *'stance in relation to policy and public affairs'* is now inadequate. Halsey suggests the College has become *'dogged by a kind of anti-intellectualism'*. *'The persistent tendency is to isolate and disregard general theory'*, he complains. *'The pervasive mood is empirical, pragmatic, tacitly social democratic, arithmetic and historical. The bias of substance as distinct from method is a complementary one towards what is British and contemporary or very recent.'*

Halsey suggested that the College was suffering from what he called *'parochialism'*. *'We are all in favour of cosmopolitan theorists with wide historical knowledge, mathematical competence and deep philosophical sophistication. But we do not elect them. Or when we do they do not dwell happily among is. John Plamenatz was gently alienated from the College. Brian Barry was chronically cross with us. Amartya Sen was puzzled and frustrated by our collective suspicion of philosophical speculation.'* Halsey has suggested that the three subject group system at Nuffield should be abolished. He wants it to be replaced by *ad hoc* groups that would be encouraged to emerge through a more unitary approach to the election of Fellows of all kinds, as well as Students by the whole of the College's Governing Body, advised by committees who would propose recommended candidates to the higher authority.

More than most College Fellows, Halsey has always taken a broader view of the purposes of Nuffield. In an internal debate during the early 1980s, he proposed some radical reforms. He wanted Nuffield to reach out not only to history and mathematics but to social anthropology and social geography. He argued that all future elections for Fellows and Students should be *'subject to the test of bilingualism'* in the social sciences. This would require a serious attempt to bring interdisciplinarism to Nuffield. *'It would mean seminars and working groups which would make it possible for every member of the politics group to understand essentially what economist Terence Gorman is arguing'*, he explained. But he regretted that at that time, there were few signs of any such bridges being built between economics and politics in the College. Halsey wanted to revive an interest in political economy as a means to encourage such a convergence of interests. He also called for a greater allocation of resources for the development of research officers and assistants.

Criticism was also levelled publicly against the prevailing ethos of a narrower quantitative approach to the social sciences in the College by Nevil Johnson in the rather bitter valedictory address that he made to colleagues in 1996. He had become a resolute opponent of what he saw as the increasing rigidity and specialisation of the three groups. Johnson said he did not even care much for the term – social science.

> *'A society is in some sense a seamless web or an intricate mosaic and it is hard to see how those questions which should concern us most can be seriously tackled and illuminated by people who know only about the dark green threads in the web or the light grey chippings in the mosaic.'*

Johnson said he was worried that those who became obsessed by their specialism would *'ultimately have no audience other than specialists like themselves.*

> *In such circumstances the various spheres of practical life of which our Statutes remind us will lose all interest in what we do. And I fear too that then the most talented and original minds in each succeeding generation will eventually be repelled by too much of Mr Dryasdust.'*

Johnson was also alarmed at what he saw as the decline of the College as a community. He feared that Nuffield had *'become more fragmented and individualised'*. There was less interchange of opinions at large across the so-called disciplinary boundaries. *'As a self governing community'*, he thought the College had grown *'less sensitive to the obvious fact that self government could only have real meaning within a real community'*. Johnson also worried that the College's three groups had turned themselves into vested interests, intent on resisting any change and seeking to perpetuate themselves through self-selection of newcomers whether as Fellows or Students. He argued that Nuffield need much more diversity in its intake and a *'more wide-ranging interpretation of the intellectual concerns'* that it pursued. As he concluded;

'If you want to avoid what some social scientists call a condition of stasis then I think that one day you will have to grasp the nettle of consolidated interests'.

Such criticisms sparked some considered responses although they have made no noticeable impression until the last few years. The most important came from the Senior Fellow, Laurence Whitehead, who has been at Nuffield for nearly forty years. It is clear that any changes that were to be carried through would have to be consistent with the purposes of the College Charter. But here again we return to that eternal conundrum about what Nuffield really stands for. It is, as always, a question of trying to balance or reconcile what look like divergent identities. The College is not exclusively a research institute but it has always been committed to research. It was not established as a teaching College but increasingly teaching has grown more important within its walls as post graduate studies have increased in importance, particularly with the rise and rise of the M Phil. Nor can Nuffield seek any monopolistic position in Oxford social studies, as the wider University has begun to devote more attention and resources to such developments.

One genuine difficulty which has always posed dilemmas for the College has been the relatively low priority given to the teaching of the social sciences at undergraduate level in Oxford. It is still impossible to secure a separate honours BA degree in economics or sociology or politics. PPE remains still the University's flagship although it is now possible to specialise overwhelmingly on politics or economics. But for those coming to the College from Oxford as graduates, it is necessary to specialise more rigorously in one of those subjects before going on to research for a doctorate. Any move to broaden the College intake but still maintain a restriction on maximum numbers would inevitably 'dilute' Nuffield's 'common core of interest' and discourage the kind of interdisciplinarity that is increasingly being called for.

Did the College miss a number of opportunities after 1979 to move in new directions? There is no clear cut answer to this. It is true that Nuffield displayed little interest in making a positive response to the rising importance of management and business studies in British higher education. Warden Chester himself had been determined to keep both of those particular subjects out of the College. His attitude was shared by every Warden in the College's history. The more recent creation of the Saïd Business School, opposite the railway station, attracts those who are interested in coming to the University to study business. But Nuffield has shown no interest in reaching out to business studies. Some have suggested this was a strategic mistake.

Nor did the College display any consistent interest in how social science research could respond and help to meet the needs and demands of the policy-makers although there were always some notable exceptions to this attitude. Increasingly it was to be in independent London-based think-tanks such as the Institute for Public Policy Research, the Social Market Foundation and the Institute for Fiscal Studies, as well as academic institutes like the LSE's Centre for Economic Performance where the current Warden when he was a Fellow worked in close and successful collaboration with Lord Layard, that were prominent in the analysis of contemporary economic and social issues.

Key public policy areas crying out for social science research at Nuffield were not considered. Back in the 1960s the College once had a distinguished Fellow in criminology – Nigel Walker. But after his retirement nobody replaced him in that particular area of study. Nuffield appears to have decided to focus its formidable resources on a number of key interests. Of course, it would be unrealistic to expect the College to try and cover the whole, wide spectrum of the social sciences. Its deliberate decision not to expand its size necessitated focus and specialisation. Nuffield was never seduced by the contemporary attractions of cultural and media studies, although it is perhaps a pity that the sociology of gender also seems to have been absent from the College's academic priorities. Nuffield could never be accused of becoming opportunistic and susceptible to transient trends. The serious, academic study of the modern world means a good deal more than responding instantly to newspaper headlines or the obsessions of increasingly populist and value-free politicians, desperate for electoral success.

Nuffield's Achievements in the Global Age

It would be quite wrong to neglect or denigrate the more positive consequences of the College's general attitude to the social sciences which have grown more evident during the past thirty years since Norman Chester's retirement. The most admirable has been Nuffield's consistent refusal to compromise its own academic independence and autonomy in response to corporate and public policy pressures. Nowadays too many academic institutions in Britain seem increasingly anxious to collaborate with outside commercial interests in the funding and implementation of research projects. The current government even appears eager to encourage private companies not only to fund more of the needs of higher education, but to formulate what curriculum and subjects should be taught in universities and other institutions. The Benthamite spirit of utilitarianism is stalking many campuses. It looks set to grow and become less easy to resist in the future. This does not appear to be true of Nuffield, at least not at present, thanks perhaps to its continuing strong financial base and equally to its firm tradition of academic freedom.

There is, however, another important reason for the College's apparent imperviousness to the current disquieting trends of commericalism and commodification that first began to appear in higher education during the 1980s. Nuffield is now heavily international in both in its ethos and interests. More than half of the research Student intake in 2008 has come from overseas, especially from countries within the European Union as well as the United States and the rest of the English-speaking world. Many of the Students are helped in their funding from College resources. Most are not constrained or inhibited by parochial British academic concerns. Their researches range widely with many Students engaged in examining problems and topics that stretch far beyond the national boundaries of Britain. Nuffield has perhaps not been as forthright as it should have been during recent years in emphasising this important international perspective in its diverse activities. If it wants to ensure it has a successful future as a post-graduate research College in Oxford, it must rely on its ability to refine and advance the global dimension of its concerns, consistent with its already existing expertise. But Nuffield is bound to face increasingly stiff competition from other parts of Oxford University as more colleges develop their own graduate facilities and the recently-formed University Departments acquire more power and authority in relation to the colleges.

A leading enthusiast for Nuffield's internationalist strategy has always been its Senior Fellow, Laurence Whitehead. For most of his academic career at the College he has been a respected specialist in the politics of Latin America and in particular of Brazil, Mexico, Bolivia and Chile. Recently, Whitehead has spent much of his time studying the international dimensions and comparative politics of globalisation. He is currently co-editing, with Desmond King, a comparative book on the democratisation of the United States, based on conference papers. Whitehead has also researched and co-ordinated a large cross-regional study of relations between the state, the market and democracy in east Asia and Latin America. His work, he explains has *'involved a balanced evaluation of the relative strengths and limitations of political development in those two regions of the world with an increasing mutual recognition of their problems'*.

Whitehead's most substantial volume, *Democratization: Theory and Experience*, was published in 2002. The introduction starts with a quotation from the American political thinker Hannah Arendt. *'Events past and present are the true, the only reliable teachers of political scientists. Once such an event (as the spontaneous uprising in Hungary in 1956) has happened, every policy, theory and forecast of future potentialities needs re-examination.'* In Whitehead's opinion this aphorism from Arendt provides an *'underlying truth'* that is applicable even to the post-Soviet world after the end of the Cold War. But his own interest in the democratisation process began with what he regards as the real turning point – the violent overthrow of Salvador Allende's left-wing government in Chile in September 1973 by the army and the creation of a brutal dictatorship led by General Augusto Pinochet. As Whitehead explains, shortly after that bloody coup in Chile democracy returned to Portugal after nearly half a century of dictatorship, and this was followed by freedom's advance once more in Greece, Spain and Peru. At first the democratisation process may have looked marginal and only a minor and limited area for academic study. But in the 1980s and 1990s other countries moved from tyranny to democracy – even unlikely ones like South Africa, Albania, Cambodia and East Timor. Whitehead's study of the process of democratisation is rooted in theory and history. As he argues, his 2002 book makes a case for *'useful knowledge, practical reason and an 'interpretative' approach to the understanding of democratisation processes'*. Whitehead recognises his analysis is controversial among many modern social scientists. But his key work is concerned with the confrontations between theory and experience that characterise the process of democratisation. Whitehead sees democratisation as a *'complex, dynamic and open ended process'*. He concluded his book by arguing that *'diversity, adaptability and deliberation are all its troublesome characteristics'* and these *'tend to get screened out of the more rigorous variants of social science theorizing'*. But Whitehead adds *'they are also characteristics that can flourish in a context of democratisation and that help account for its resilience and also its normative appeal'*.

In the past, Whitehead may have seen himself as rather a marginal figure in both his area-study research and less than pure commitment to social science orthodoxies. Although not a trenchant critic of quantification, he has always taken a pragmatic but principled view of modern studies. Above all, Whitehead recognises the limitations of the quantitative approach and he is probably well aware of what the historian H A L Fisher once called *'the contingent and the unforeseen'* in human affairs that can wreck the grandest of social theories by gritty and unwelcome surprises.

Some recent fellowship appointments suggest that comparative empirical research is growing more important in the College, at least among those who belong to the politics group. Desmond King who joined Nuffield in 2002 from a Fellowship in politics at St Johns College and is at present Mellon Professor of American Government as Byron Shafer's replacement. A good example of this trend, King is a prolific writer on American politics, particularly on the tangled issues of race and national identity. His two books, *The Liberty of Strangers* and *Separate and Unequal*, are widely respected on both sides of the Atlantic. But he has also written about current labour market policies in democratic western societies. King describes himself in his approach to political science as an *'historical institutionalist'*. He writes lucidly without any resort to mind-numbing jargon. Much of his most important work is grounded in exhaustive archival research, but it is also contained within an important theoretical framework that is convincing and relevant to non-academics, particularly to the public policy makers. His study of British and American social policy towards the unemployed, *Actively Seeking Work? The Politics of Unemployment and Welfare Policy in Britain and the United States* (1995), provided a forceful analysis of the uses of state coercion to deal with the jobless made by democratic governments in recent times to deal with the jobless. King links his public policy concerns with an interest in the politics of eugenics and its importance for the evolution of contemporary progressive democratic politics. He makes a persuasive case for a more empirically-rooted political science that uses and does not ignore or misuse history. His emphasis on institutions bedded in history is long overdue. He relates public-policy institutions to the realities of the world and not to the construction of abstract models. In doing so he challenges the behaviourialist and mathematical approach to politics both in the College and elsewhere.

Diego Gambetta, who came to Nuffield as a Fellow in 2003, is another distinguished Official Fellow in the College who reflects a closer relationship between the social and the political is. His sociological research interests have already broken new ground. In 2005 Gambetta's edited volume on suicide missions was published. It looks at some of the groups who now make the headlines around the world for their murderous activities in the Middle East and beyond – Al Qaeda, the Tamil Tigers, Palestinian groups like Hamas and Hezbollah and the Japanese kamikaze. In his foreword to the book, Gambetta explained the approach of he and his colleagues to *'the defining act of political violence of our age'* was motivated not only by *'an intense and dispassionate interest in the explanatory challenges it poses to social scientists'* but also by *'their dissatisfaction with the simplistic or ideological interpretations of it that were being proposed'*. Gambetta insists that to make sense of the suicide missions it is necessary *'to rely on solid, wide ranging empirical evidence and to identify the theoretical questions that we should meaningfully ask about them'*.

Gambetta has also written a fascinating comparative study about how taxi drivers in Belfast and New York assess the trustworthiness of their passengers. Early research by Gambetta was concerned with the activities of the Italian Mafia. The wide range of his academic interests has brought freshness to Nuffield sociology. It is a further sign of growing interest among the Fellows in the processes of globalisation, and, in his case, the politics and sociology of contemporary terrorism.

Two recent arrivals in the College politics group reflect the growth of interest in comparative political studies in the College. Nancy Bermeo came to Nuffield from Princeton University in 2007. Her primary interest is in the politics of regime change, the effects of war on the emergence of new democracies and the importance of inequality in the struggle for democracy. Gwendolyn Sasse joined the College, from the LSE's European Institute, as a Professorial Fellow and Reader in Comparative Politics, at the same time. She specialises mainly in the politics of central and eastern Europe. Sasse's published work includes studies of ethnicity and territory in regional conflicts in parts of the former Soviet Union, notably the Ukraine. It is gratifying to see two women of such high academic calibre becoming Nuffield Fellows. But equally their presence in the College may help to focus more attention than in the recent past on the importance of area studies as a means of integrating politics, economics and sociology in a relevant way. It suggests that opportunities for greater diversity in the composition of the Fellowship are not as limited as it may once have been thought.

The appointment of a former Student David Soskice for a seven-year University research professorship is perhaps a further sign that Nuffield may be developing its interests in contemporary politics in more comparative directions. Soskice's co-edited volume with Peter Hall of Harvard University, *The Varieties of Capitalism*, caused quite a stir in academic circles when it was published a few years ago. It is true that in the search for explanations of why different democratic political economies have pursued different economic and social policies, the authors ignored modern history. But at least they engaged with the often complex and always fluid interconnection between contemporary politics and economics that have helped to make Germany, Sweden and other northern European countries less susceptible to the kind of economic individualistic neo-liberalism dominant in the United States, and to a lesser extent, Britain.

A further recent appointment as Senior Research Fellow will strengthen the comparative institutional approach to politics in the College. Kathleen Thelen is a professor at Northwestern University in the United States with a high reputation in Europe for her published work on the political economies of Germany and Sweden.

A number of Fellows elected to the College some time ago continue to strengthen the politics group. These include John Darwin, Reader in Commonwealth history. His book, *After Tamerlane: The Global History of Empire* published in 2007 was widely praised by reviewers. The economic history Fellow, Robert Allen, is doing pioneering work on data sets on prices and wages for the past five centuries. He is also researching living standards in India and China before industrialisation, as well as a study on the origins of the industrial revolution in Britain.

178

David Miller, the College's distinguished political theorist since 1979, is now also taking a close interest in international questions. In 2007 he wrote a thoughtful book, *National Responsibility and Global Justice*, that seeks to relate nation-state responsibilities to the demands for justice and well-being that are coming from the wider developing world. In his analysis of the interconnection between rights and responsibilities at national and international level, Miller has made an important contribution to a growing debate about the political nature of what we perhaps too loosely call globalisation. In bringing his past work as a theorist to such urgent practical matters, Miller is returning to the College's core purposes.

International relations as an academic subject first arrived in the College in 1986. The longest serving Nuffield Fellow in this field was Andrew Hurrell, who was elected to the Montague Burton Chair in International Relations in 2007 and moved to Balliol College, after over twenty years at Nuffield. However, his latest discursive and important theoretical study, *On Global Order: Power, Values and the Constitution of International Society*, published in 2007 was mainly researched and written at the College. In this closely-argued book, Hurrell draws on a range of political theorists including John Rawls and Jürgen Habermas, to set out his ideas of how our world can be governed more effectively through the complex interplay of international, national and civil society institutions. Hurrell's analysis of what he calls the international society seeks to link the pursuit of global political and social justice within an unequal and unstable world. He concludes that *'the ethical claims of international society rest on the contention that such a society continues to be the most stable set of globally institutionalized political processes by which norms and rules can be negotiated on the basis of dialogue and consent rather than simply being imposed by the most powerful'*. But Hurrell is a realist. *'There is very little reason for supposing that progress in the direction of moral accessibility, institutional stability or more balanced and equitable forms of political agency is likely to be easy. It may not be possible at all.'* However, he ends his thoughtful book by suggesting what he is advocating remains of crucial importance for international politics. As he notes, *'Understanding how the rope bridge may be spun out across the canyon is central both to the chances of world order in the twenty-first century and to the promotion of global social justice'.*

The other College Fellow who is researching international politics is Yuen Foong Khong. He has a particular interest in American foreign policy and politics in the Asia- Pacific region.

These examples of recent research at Nuffield by some of the politics Fellows indicates that they are making important scholarly contributions to knowledge that fall outside Nuffield's core preoccupations with quantification and model-building. In the recent past they have tended to plough their own individual furrows and some of them have felt marginalised as a result. Encouraging a greater sense of collegiality among the politics Fellows around a broader agenda of realism and positivism would be a welcome development if it began to open up Nuffield to the wider community, because the social sciences in Britain need to grow more, not less, relevant to public policy-making, or just to an understanding of the world in which we all have to live.

The Future of the College – Prescriptions for Change

Nuffield does not need to undergo any radical shift of direction in the future to renew its already established role in social research, but it needs to play to some of its existing strengths. In doing so, it could relate them much more closely to the College's original purposes as enshrined in its own ambitious Statutes. In other words, Nuffield might develop a coherent and credible strategy that could enable it once more to engage more closely with the outside world in the application of the social sciences to meet the formidable political, social and economic challenges posed by globalisation in its many forms. In his latest book, David Miller writes, *'Human beings are needy and vulnerable creatures who cannot live decent, let alone flourishing lives unless they are given at least a minimum bundle of freedoms, opportunities and resources. They must have freedom to think and act, the opportunity to learn and work and the resources to feed and clothe themselves. When people lack these conditions, it seems that those who are better endowed have obligations of justice to help provide them.*

180

On the other hand, human beings are choosing agents who must take responsibility for their own lives. This means they should be allowed to enjoy the benefits of success but it also means that they must bear the burdens of failure. And where their actions impose costs on others, they should be held liable for those costs, which entails in some cases making redress to the people whose interests they have damaged'.

Nuffield's academic future should be as an important, self confident, widely recognised and respected international centre for the social sciences as they seek in their different ways to meet the challenges posed by our dangerous and turbulent world. But growing both more international and broader in its social science interests does not lessen the urgent need for greater interdisciplinary activity inside the College. On the contrary, it strengthens the demand for a much more unitary approach based on Nuffield's already existing academic strengths. There are some welcome signs that this is beginning to happen under the current Warden, Steve Nickell. He is moving in this direction through his evident determination to encourage interdisciplinary projects that will bring the College's economists, sociologists and political scientists together for their mutual benefit. The recent initiative in experimental social science is the first example. None of this means that the quantitative approach to the social sciences should be downgraded or neglected. On the contrary, the College, under the influence of John Goldthorpe and Anthony Heath has won an international reputation for the sophistication of its analysis of class formation and social mobility. This achievement should be built on and strengthened even further.

But there is a need for the College to re-evaluate what it stands for today. It should re-examine the role of the Visiting Fellows and give them more to do, perhaps through holding more seminars, workshops and conferences in which they can participate with Fellows and Students. Nuffield should produce a series of pamphlets aimed at the policy-makers and the wider informed public on issues of contemporary importance where the College's existing expertise can be utilised effectively. This does not mean any return to the 'golden age'. That period has long gone. But it might mean some different kind of reconnection between the academic and the non-academic which was, after all, one of the important reasons why the College was founded in the first place.

Nuffield also needs to reassess itself in relation to the newly formed social studies departments in the University. Its Fellows are dominant in those departments and they are setting the agenda. But inevitably these new bodies, which cut across the colleges, are potentially rival centres of academic power and influence. Nuffield will have to establish a new relationship with them. It cannot take them over even if it wished to do so. On the other hand, it can no longer act as a competitor. It is going to take exceptional diplomacy to reconcile the College and the University departments in 'modern' studies. But it needs to be done. Warden Nickell has some bold plans to establish Nuffield and its immediate area as a focus for social studies in Oxford University. A cluster that stretches from the College to the Saïd Business School may still be far away and not yet on the drawing board. But this could be an exciting future for the social sciences in the University in the next decade.

It might be more effectively achieved if Nuffield could discover a new grand narrative for its future existence that can integrate its various parts together as a totality around a common programme of social research. An elegant justification for such a possible way forward can be found in the recent writings of that political economist of international renown, Amartya Sen, later Master of Trinity College, Cambridge and a Nobel Prize winner. Sen was Professor of development economics and a Nuffield Professorial Fellow from 1977 until 1980. Christopher Bliss believes – like many others – that Sen is the *'greatest political economist of his generation'. 'His work demonstrates that the combination of economics with political analysis and engagement need not result in loose theorising.'* Sen's finest personal contributions to economics included his analysis of the Bengal Famine of the early 1940s. But his lasting contribution to economics was to cast doubt on the achievements of the Chinese Model under Communism, compared with India's own economic experience during the same period from the 1950s until the 1980s. *'Before the devastating consequences of Chairman Mao's Great Leap Forward were known, Sen questioned this simplistic view'*, writes Bliss. *'He argued in particular that the fact that India avoided any mass mortality due to famine since its independence can be attributed to India's generally democratic and open society and its free press. In contrast, millions of Chinese died in the famines caused by the Great Leap Forward without the world knowing. Sen dared to write this when it was not widely accepted, certainly not on the political left. Subsequently the estimates of mortality which he speculated have been shown to be underestimates.'*

But perhaps Sen's greatest achievement, which is of relevance to this personal history of Nuffield, lies in his evaluation of poverty and inequality. He is *'no nationalist partisan'* argues Bliss and instances Sen's comparative work on poorly developed Africa compared with relatively better performing India. Sen found that female infant life expectancy was lower in his own country than it was in Africa. The *'missing women'* is now the focus for research interests and policy making everywhere and that includes the World Bank.

This brief history of Nuffield College is concluding with an appreciation of Sen because, more than any other academic who has carried out research within its walls, he is an exemplar of the importance of a unitary approach to the study of the social sciences and how they can become relevant again to an understanding of our shattered world. Of course, Sen's own background suggests his focus on global questions of freedom and development is rooted in his own past as a young boy growing up in post-independence India. *'For all his broad international reach, Sen is completely a product of Bengal'*, Bliss points out. *'His broad philosophical and rigorous intellectual approach reflects the excitement of the open, culturally mixed, coastal culture of modern Bengal.'*

In the preface to his book *Development As Freedom* published in 1999, Sen wrote a moving justification for the primacy of economics in the research and teaching of 'modern' studies. The volume was based on a lecture series he gave to the World Bank. But economics alone, he argued, was not enough. Sen provides us with a cogent testament to the important interconnectedness that exists in the real world between economics, politics and sociology. As he wrote; *'We live in a world of unprecedented opulence, of a kind that would have been hard even to imagine a century or two ago. There have also been some remarkable changes beyond the economic sphere. The twentieth century established democratic and participatory governance as the pre-eminent model of political organisation. Concepts of human rights and political liberty are now over much a part of the prevailing rhetoric. People live much longer, on the average, than ever before. Also, the different regions of the globe are now more closely linked than they have ever been. This is so not only in the fields of trade, commerce and communication but also in terms of interactive ideas and ideals.'*

Sen contrasted this optimistic idealistic but partial picture of the present with the dark underside of our world. *'And yet we also live in a world with remarkable deprivation, destitution and oppression. There are many new problems as well as old ones, including persistence of poverty and unfulfilled elementary needs, occurrence of famines and widespread hunger, violation of elementary political freedoms as well as basic liberties, extensive neglect of the interests and agency of women, and worsening threats to our environment and to the sustainability of our economic and social lives. Many of these deprivations can be observed, in one form or another, in rich countries as well as poor ones.'*

Sen then brought the two pictures of the world together and integrated them into his strategic thoughts of what needs to be done. *'Overcoming these problems is a central part of the exercise of development. We have to recognise the role of freedom of different kinds in countering these afflictions. Indeed, individual agency is ultimately central to addressing these deprivations. On the other hand, the freedom of agency that we individually have is inescapably qualified and constrained by the social, political and economic opportunities that are available to us. There is a deep complementarity between individual agency and social arrangements. To counter the problems we face we have to see individual freedom as a social commitment.'*

Sen's inspiring words, express in the language of the twenty-first century what Lindsay and the other College pioneers were seeking to explain and justify seventy years ago in their thoughts of what the ultimate purposes of Nuffield College should be. Sen was not, of course, thinking of the College or any other academic institution in what he wrote but in his words he articulates the importance of what ought to be the more integrated or connective nature of the social sciences in how they should make their measured responses to the innumerable challenges of our world. Sen is the kind of broad-based Fellow that the College needs to see more of in the future. The pursuit of human freedom through sustainable economic development is a noble project that provides the social sciences with a broader and idealistic purpose. A commitment to this objective does not mean that Nuffield should turn itself into a narrowly focused institution with an ideological or even a reformist agenda that is beholden to any particular government or pressure group. On the contrary, the College must always remain free of corporate or government pressures and influences, as it has done in the past. It should continue to assert its academic independence and remain critical of conventional wisdom and orthodoxies while being sensitively aware of both social and economic problems. The idealistic hopes of 1937 may not have been realised; perhaps they never could be in the confines of a single College or even a University. They were always too vague and too ambitious, perhaps even Utopian. But what concerned Lindsay and to a lesser extent Lord Nuffield still remains relevant for the College today as it celebrates the fiftieth anniversary of the granting of its Royal Charter. The harnessing of the social sciences, in all their complexities and diversity, to the betterment and enlightenment of humanity is still a cause worth fighting for. Nuffield should be at the epicentre of such an endeavour in the name of rationalism, empiricism and devotion to evidence-based research. The next fifty years will determine whether the College can live up to its original purposes and make a genuine difference to the freedom and prosperity of humanity.

Appendices

College Office Holders – Eminences – Achievements – Miscellany – Statistics

1: College Officers

Founder
1937-63 Viscount
Nuffield

Visitor
1958 Lord Evershed
1962 Lord Denning
1982 Sir John (Lord)
Donaldson
1992 Sir Thomas
Bingham
1996 Lord Woolf
1999 Lord Phillips
2005 Sir Anthony
Clarke

Warden
1938 (Sir) Harold
Butler
1945 Sir Henry Clay
1949 Alexander
Loveday
1954 (Sir) Norman
Chester
1978 Michael Brock
1988 Sir David Cox
1994 Sir Tony
Atkinson
2006 Steve Nickell

Sub-Warden
1942-43 G.D.H.
Cole

Senior Fellow
1938 (Dame)
Margery Perham
1963 Herbert Frankel
1971 Francis Seton
1987 David Butler
1992 James Mirrlees
1995 Laurence
Whitehead

Domestic Bursar
1954 Hugh Clegg
1958 Bryan Keith-
Lucas
1964 Francis Seton
1965 Freddie
Madden
1966 David
Fieldhouse
1976 David Butler
1977 Kenneth
Macdonald
1979 Bob Tricker
1982-89 A.H. Halsey

Full-time Bursar
1989 Simon Porter
1996 Gwilym Hughes

Investment Bursar
1958-64 Sir Donald
MacDougall
1958-65 Ian Little
1963-76 Uwe
Kitzinger
1965-67 Peter
Oppenheimer
1967-70 Ian Little
1970-79 John
Flemming
1973-75 Peter
Oppenheimer
1975-78 Laurence
Whitehead
1978-83 Christopher
Bliss
1980-87 Maurice
Scott
1986-87 John Vickers
1986-88 Christopher
Bliss
1988-89 Laurence
Whitehead

1990-92 Ian Little
1992-93 Christopher
Bliss
1994-98 Richard
Spady
1995-95 Christopher
Bliss
1996-00 Laurence
Whitehead
1997-00 Hyun Shin
2000-02 Kevin
Roberts
2000-02 John
Muellbauer
2002-06 Iain McLean
2006-08 Christopher
Bliss
2006- Bob Allen

Dean of Degrees
1958 Freddie
Madden
1973 Denys Munby
1976 John Joliffe
1982 Richard Mayou
1988 Noel Gale
2001 Meir Yaish
2002 Jim Engle-
Warnick
2003 Andrew Hurrell
2004 Mark Kayser
2005 Chris Bowdler
2006 Roland Meeks
2007 Maria
Sobolewska

**Keeper of the
Gardens**
1958 John Plamenatz
1967 A.H. Halsey
1989 Nevil Johnson
1997 Anthony Heath

Chairman of SCR
1959 Philip Williams
1963 Freddie
Madden
1973 Francis Seton
1979 David Butler
1985 Jim Sharpe
1986 Chris Harris
1989 Ray Fitzpatrick
1999 Lucy Carpenter
2006 David Miller
2007 Ray Duch

Dean
1956 David Butler
1964 Chris Winsten
1968 Philip Williams
1972 Aubrey
Silberston
1978 Max Hartwell
1980 Barry Supple
1981 Eric Batstone
1987 Ray Fitzpatrick

Senior Tutor
1956 David Butler
1964 Chris Winsten
1968 Brian Barry
1969 John Flemming
1970 Laurence
Whitehead
1978 Clyde Mitchell
1980 David Miller
1986 Duncan Gallie
1990 David Miller
1991 John Darwin
1996 Clive Payne
2001 Jeremy
Richardson
2003 Geoffrey
Evans

Fellow Librarian	Proctor or Assessor	1969 Philippa	Resident Caretaker
1950 Kenneth	1967-8 Uwe	Gibson	1976 Vic Sylvester
Robinson	Kitzinger	1976 Margaret	1988 Derek
1957 Max Hartwell	1977-8 John	Hunt	Lambert
1975 Nevil Johnson	Flemming	1986 Marion Rogers	1998 Neville Powell
1997 John	1988-9 David Miller	2001 Lucy Chevis	2007 Rod Oakey
Goldthorpe		2003 Lin Sorrell	
2000 Duncan Gallie	On General Board		Chef
	Sir Norman Chester	Academic	1958 Ken Hudson
Librarian	Michael Brock	Administrator	1987 Vito Campo
1946 Bridget Bertie	Freddie Madden	2001 Marion Rogers	1995 Stephen
1960 Christine	A.H. Halsey	2004 Stephanie	Ramli-Davies
Kennedy	Richard Mayou	Wright	1997 Ross Boffin
1994 James Legg			
2001 Elizabeth	On Hebdomadal	Chief Secretary	
Martin	Council	1953 Jean	Butler
	Michael Brock	Brotherhood	1958 Stan Rogers
Chaplain	A.H. Halsey	1989 Maureen	1962 Gerry Smith
1947 Ray Lee		Baker	1984 Tom Hook
1969 Philip Martin	Warden's Secretary		1992 Oliver Gibbs
1971 Robert Brown	1948 Susan Prior	Head Porter	2001 Daniel Lawson
1984 Chris Brice	1954 Kate Skey	1958-76 Tom Cross	
1986 Helen Cunliffe	1958 Jill Hine		
1989 Margaret Yee	1961 Anne Gowers	Handy Man	
	1963 Margaret	1958-76 Charlie	
	Hunt	Wheeler	

2: College Notables

Vice-Chancellors

Douglas Anglin	Zambia
Sir George Bain	Belfast
Sir Ivor Crewe	Essex
Sir Roderick Floud	Guildhall, London Metropolitan
Alan Gilbert	Melbourne, Manchester
Kenneth Inglis	New Guinea
Kenneth Robinson	Hong Kong
Harry Rowen	Rand Corporation
Ron Watts	Queens, Ontario
Glenn Willson	Murdoch, WA
	Goldsmith's
Sir Charles Wilson	Leicester, Glasgow

College Heads

Sir Ivor Crewe	University College
John Flemming	Wadham College
Jean Floud	Newnham College
Sir Roderick Floud	London Guildhall
John Kay	LBS
Uwe Kitzinger	Templeton College
Robin Matthews	Clare College
Sir Derek Morris	Oriel College
George Richardson	Keble College
John Rowett	Rhodes House
Amartya Sen	Trinity, Cambridge
Richard Smethurst	Worcester College
Barry Supple	St. Catherine's, Cambridge
Richard Trainor	King's College, London
Sir John Vickers	All Souls

MPs
Frederick Mulley 1950-83
Brian Walden 1964-76
Stanley Henig 1966-70
Alan Beith 1973-
Austin Mitchell 1977-
Andrew Tyrie 1997-
Martin Linton 1997-
Caroline Jackson (MEP) 1984-

Nobel Prize-Winners
Sir John Hicks
Sir James Mirrlees
Amartya Sen

Reith Lecturers
Dame Margery Perham
Alj Mazrui
A.H. Halsey

Other Public Figures
Sir Franklin Berman
Sir Ian Byatt
Martin Feldstein
Alexandre Lamfalussy
Sir Gus O'Donnell
Sir Alan Walters

Other Elected Politicians
Kofi Busia (Ghana)
Turban Feyzoglu (Turkey)
Bemard Chidzero (Zimbabwe)
Manmohan Singh (India)
Kamal Hossain (Bangladesh)
Kalu Ezera (Nigeria)
Harold Edwards (Australia)
Geoff Gallup (West Australia)

Peers
Donald Chapman
William McCarthy
Frederick Mulley
Robert Skidelsky
Norman Warner
Bernard Donoughue
Patricia Hollis
Matthew Oakeshott
William Wallace
Andrew Adonis
Nick Stern

The British Academy

FBAs 2007	No. in Section	Nuffield Links
Economics	56	20
Politics	30	10
Sociology	39	7

188

3: Select Publications

A Few of the Books or Articles Written in the College
Robert Allen, *Enclosure and the Yeoman* (1992)
Philippe Aghion et al, *Endogenous Growth Theory* (1998)
Philip Andrews, *Manufacturing Business* (1949)
Brian Barry, *Sociologists, Economists and Democracy* (1970)
Eric Batstone, *Reform of Workplace Industrial Relations* (1988)
Christopher Bliss, *Capital Mobility Convergence Clubs and Long-Run Economic Growth* (1995)
Michael Brock et al, *History of the University of Oxford Vols.6&7 1800-1914* (1997, 2000)
David Butler and Donald Stokes, *Political Change in Britain* (1969)
Norman Chester, *The Nationalisation of British Industry* (1975)
Hugh Clegg et al, *A History of British Trade Unions Since 1889* (1964-1994)
Max Corden, *Trade Policy and Economic Welfare* (1974)
David Cox, *Principles of Statistical Inference* (2006)
John Darwin, *After Tamerlane: the Global History of Empire since 1405* (2007)
Ray Duch and Randy Stevenson, *The Economic Vote: How Political and Economic Institutions Condition Election Results* (2008)
Geoff Evans et al, *The End of Class Politics* (1999)
Martin Feldstein, *Economic Analysis for Health Service Efficiency* (1967)
David Fieldhouse, *Economics and Empire* (1973)
David Firth, 'Robust Models in Probability Sampling' *JRSS* (1998)
John Flemming, *Inflation* (1976)
Jean Floud, *Dangerousness and Criminal Justice* (1981)
Herbert Frankel, *Money: Two Philosophies* (1977)
Noel Gale, *Bronze Age Trade in the Aegean* (2001)
Duncan Gallie et al, *Restructuring the Employment Relationship* (1998)
John Goldthorpe, *On Sociology* (2007)
Terence Gorman et al, *Doing Economics Economically*
A.H. Halsey, *A History of Sociology in Britain* (2004)
Max Hartwell, *The Industrial Revolution and Economic Growth* (1971)
Anthony Heath et al, *How Britain Votes* (1985)
Peter Hedström, *Dissecting the Social* (2005)
David Hendry, *Dynamic Econometrics* (1995)
John Hicks, *A Contribution to the Theory of the Trade Cycle* (1950)
Andrew Hurrell, *On Global Order: Power Values and the Constitution of International Society* (2007)
Nevil Johnson, *In Search of the Constitution* (1977)
Yuen Khong, *Analogies at War: Munich, Korea, Dien Bien Phu and the Vietnam Decisions* (1997)
Paul Klemperer, *Auctions: Theory and Practice* (2004)
Uwe Kitzinger, *Diplomacy and Persuasion: How Britain Joined the Common Market* (1973)
Ian Little, *A Critique of Welfare Economics* (1950)

Iain McLean, *Fixing the Boundaries* (1996)

Donald MacDougall, *The World Dollar Problem* (1957)

A.F. Madden et al, *Constitutional History of the British Empire and Commonwealth* (1984-99)

Gordon Marshall, *Presbyteries and Profits* (1980)

Meg Meyer and Paul Klemperer, 'Supply Function Equilibria in Oligopoly under Uncertainty', *Econometrica* (1989)

David Miller, *On Nationality* (1995)

Jim Mirrlees and Ian Little, *Project Appraisal and Planning for Developing Countries* (1974)

Clyde Mitchell, *Cities, Society and Social Perception* (1987)

John Muellbauer et al, *Economics and Consumer Behaviour* (1980)

Stephen Nickell et al, *Unemployment: Macroeconomic Performance and the Labour Market* (1991)

Bent Nielsen and David Hendry, *On the Principles of Economic Modeling* (2007)

Avner Offer, 'Between the Gift and the Market: the Economy of Regard' *Economic History Review* (1997)

Clive Payne, *Election Forecasting in the UK: the BBC's Experience* (2003)

Margery Perham, *Lugard* (1956-60)

John Plamenatz, *Man and Society* (1963)

Kevin Roberts, 'The Characterisation of Implementable Choice Rules' *Aggregation and Revelation of Preferences* (1979)

Amartya Sen, *Poverty and Famines* (1981)

Maurice Scott, *A New View of Economic Growth* (1989)

Byron Shafer, *The Two Majorities and the Puzzle of Modern American Politics* (2003)

L.J. Sharpe and K. Newton, *Does Politics Matter?* (1984)

Richard Spady et al, 'Information Theoretic Approaches to Inference in Moment-Condition Models', *Econometrica (1998)*

John Vickers et al, *Privatization: An Economic Analysis* (1988)

Nigel Walker, *Crime, Courts and Figures* (1971)

Laurence Whitehead, *Democratization: Theory and Experience* (2002)

Philip Williams, *Crisis and Compromise* (1964)

Vincent Wright, *The Government and Politics of France* (1978)

Peyton Young, *Individual Strategy and Social Structure* (1998)

4: A Selection of Journals Edited in College

Biometrica (Cox 1988-94)

Economic History Review (Hartwell 1960-68)

Econometrics Journal (Shephard 1988-2003)

Economic Journal (Flemming 1976-80, Klemperer 2000-2004, Bliss 1996-2004)

Electoral Studies (Butler 1982-92, McLean 1992-99, Evans 1999-)

Journal of Common Market Studies (Kitzinger 1962-76)

Journal of Latin American Studies (Whitehead 1990-)

Journal of the Royal Statistical Society A (Payne 1999-2002)

Journal of the Royal Statistical Society B (Firth 1998-2002)

Oxford Bulletin of Economics and Statistics (Nickell 1984-98, Hendry 1982-98)

Oxford Review of Education (Halsey 1970-2004)
Political Studies (Sharpe 1976-82)
Public Administration (Chester 1943-66, Johnson 1966-81)
Rand Journal of Economics (Klemperer 1993-1999)
Review of Economic Studies (Klemperer 1989-97, Shin 1998-2003)
Review of International Studies (Vincent 1986-89)
Sociology (Goldthorpe 1970-73)
Western European Politics (Wright 1978-99)

5: Collective Projects

African Studies (1939-63)
Social Reconstruction Survey (1940-45)
Election Histories (1945-2005)
Trade Union Studies (1950-66)
Voting Studies (1961-)
Social Trends (1965-99)
Cost Benefit Analysis (1997-76)
Optimal Income: Tax (1997-73)
Social Mobility (1998-80)
Inflation (1974-76)
Imperial History (1958-99)
Social Change and Economic Life (1985-90
Econometric Modelling and Forecasting (1983-)
Labour Market Security, Unemployment and Social Exclusion (1996-)
Quality of Life (1995-)

In 1999, at least one of the PPE Tutors at 22 of the 29 traditional Oxford undergraduate Colleges was a former Nuffield Student.

6: Finance and Chronology

	Capital	Annual Budget
1958	£1,024,000	£78,644
1970	£4,564,000	£216,491
1980	£11,725,000	£533,507
1990	£47,197,000	£1,823,678
2000	£96,700,000	£4,751,780

Chronology
1937 Trust Deed signed
1938 Austen Harrison appointed architect
1939 War postpones building
1939 First Fellow appointed
1942 G.D.H. Cole as Sub-Warden
1945 First Student appointed
1949 Foundation Stone laid
1950 Staircase B and C completed
1951 Staircase D and E occupied
1954 Decision to complete building
1957 College takes over its finances
1958 Charter granted 18 April
1958 Hall opened 6 June
1958 College becomes residential
1961 Chapel consecrated
1963 Death of Lord Nuffield
1968 Mews building opened
1969 Students join in College government
1975 College retrenches in financial crisis
1982 First College computer
1987 50th Anniversary of Founding
1992 1000th Student signs register
2002 1250th Student signs register
2008 50th Charter Anniversary

7: Origins and Destinations

<u>Size of College</u>

Year	Official Fellows	Professorial Fellows	Faculty and Supernum'y	Research Fellows	Students
1950	8	8	5	3	21
1960	9	6	2	11	33
1970	11	9	4	14	41
1980	11	7	11	9	46
1990	13	9	10	20	61
2000	15	8	11	26	74
2006	11	14	9	48	59

<u>Origins and Destinations of Permanent Fellows of Nuffield</u>

Years	Schooling			University				Destination						Women
	Public	State	Overseas	Oxford	Cambridge	Other UK	Overseas	Oxford	Cambridge	Other UK	Overseas	Non academic	Nuffield	
1939-58	12	8	4	28	9	4	1	6	2	7	2	1	10	1
1958-70	6	10	3	11	2	6	4	1	4	3	5	5	8	1
1971-80	2	7	5	2	7	2	3	-	3	2	3	4	8	-
1981-90	6	10	2	6	3	6	2	2	2	3	2	2	9	2
1991-00	2	9	10	1	4	10	7	2	-	1	4	6	13	2
Total	28	44	24	48	25	28	17	11	11	16	16	18	48	6

These figures do not include Professorial and Faculty Fellows before 1958 who were also Fellows of other Colleges.

Background of Visiting Fellows of Nuffield College

	Business	Public Service	Politics	Trade Union	Media	Academic	Advisory Body	Total
1939-50	10	3	1	3	-	2	-	19
1951-60	1	4	2	1	2	1	-	13
1961-70	4	7	2	5	1	-	-	18
1971-80	4	4	1	2	3	3	-	18
1981-90	4	9	7	3	1	1	1	2
1991-00	4	8	5	6	4	-	4	26
Total (n)	31	35	16	13	11	7	5	116
Total (%)	27%	30%	14%	11%	9%	6%	4%	100%

National and Educational Origins of Nuffield Students

	UK Origin	Oxbridge Origin	Public School	Of UK Oxford	Of UK Public School	Total Number
	%	%	%	%	%	
1945-50	71	63	23	77	42	61
1951-55	45	35	15	62	39	76
1956-60	47	53	24	73	59	86
1961-65	66	53	26	70	49	110
1966-70	65	54	34	71	54	130
1971-75	68	46	27	46	43	119
1976-80	66	44	30	61	45	135
1981-85	53	38	15	49	35	130
1986-90	53	41	18	61	53	119
1991-95	48	32	12	41	32	134
1996-00	34	33	12	44	33	128

Gender and Student Admission to Nuffield College

Year	Female %
1945-50	5
1951-55	13
1956-60	11
1961-65	9
1966-70	10
1971-75	14
1976-80	19
1981-85	20
1986-90	27
1991-95	27
1996-2000	41
2001-05	53
Average %	21

Origins and destinations of Nuffield Students (1945-2000)

	U.K. Origin (%)	Female (%)	Economists (%)	Oxbridge % of UK Students	Oxbridge % of all Students	Pub. Sch. % of UK Students	Academic (%)	Public Service (%)	Business (%)	Total (n)
1945-50	71	5	41	77	63	42	74	20	7	61
1951-55	45	13	47	62	35	39	65	20	15	76
1956-60	47	11	40	73	53	59	71	21	6	86
1961-65	66	9	37	70	53	49	87	8	3	111
1966-70	65	10	37	71	54	54	73	19	4	130
1971-75	65	14	42	46	46	43	56	26	15	119
1976-80	68	19	42	61	44	45	51	26	18	135
1981-85	66	20	39	49	38	35	67	19	10	130
1986-90	53	27	38	61	41	53	69	15	13	119
1991-95	48	27	40	41	32	32	60	17	22	134
1996-00	34	41	30	44	33	33	56	16	29	128
Overall	57	19	39	58	43	47	66	18	13	1229

Occupation

Two-thirds of all Nuffield Students have moved, at least initially, from the College into university teaching. But up to 1970, the proportion was 75%, and after 1970, 60%. In 1961-5 there was a remarkable peak (87%) reflecting the sudden university expansion of the post-Robbins era.

A little under 20% have gone into public service, with a special dip when university posts were so easy to get in the 1960s. In the 1990s the lure of City salaries raised the proportion going into business from the 10% of the early days to over a quarter.

Prior Education

Until 1970, 70% of British Nuffield Students came from Oxford but by the 1990s the proportion had fallen to 40%. 43% of all Students have come from Oxford or Cambridge but the proportion fell from 50% in 1970 to 33% in the 1990s.

London (mainly LSE) provided 6% of students and other English universities 20%. Students have come from all Oxford undergraduate Colleges. But some sources stand out: Balliol 10%, Magdalen 7%, New College 6%, University 6%, St. John's 5% and Wadham 5%. Corpus 6% stands out among the smaller colleges. From Cambridge, St. John's topped the list.

Nationality

There was no chauvinism in selection. Little more than half of Nuffield Students have had British passports – 57% up to 1990 but only 41% since then. The United States provided 10% of Students, Australia and New Zealand together 6%. Western Europe has provided 8% (with the proportion increasing sharply in recent decades). Of the Students from Western Europe, Ireland has contributed 40, Germany 23, Italy 16, Spain 11, Belgium 9, France 7, Greece 7, Norway 7, Switzerland 1 and the Dutch 6. Luxembourg is the only Western European country which has never sent a student to Nuffield.

Subject Area

In the mid 1950s, the College divided academically between an Economics Group and a Politics Group; Social and Economic Historians and other less represented disciplines were usually attached to the Politics Group. But in 1959, under the impetus of Hugh Clegg and Max Hartwell, a third Group was established which, after a few years, became known as the Sociology Group.

By the 1970s it was broadly accepted that each year's intake should be roughly equally divided between the three Groups (with a small inter-disciplinary category for those who did not fit clearly into any of them). Over the life of the College, economists accounted for just under 40% of each quinquennial intake until the late 1990s when the economists fell to 30%.

Gender

The most striking trend to emerge from all these quinquennial statistics is the change from 5% women in the first tranche to 41% in the last. Indeed in 2001-2, the majority of new Students were women.

196

8: Notes on Sources

Some sources

Adeney, M., *Nuffield: A Biography* (1993)

Andrews, P. and Brunner, E., *Life of Lord Nuffield* (1955)

Butler, D. and Halsey, A.H., *Policy and Politics* (1978)

Chester, D.N., *Economics, Politics and Social Studies in Oxford* (1982)

Cole, M., *The Life of G D H Cole* (1971)

Colvin, H., *Unbuilt Oxford* (1983)

Halsey, A.H., *No Discouragement* (1992)

Halsey, A.H., *A History of Sociology in Britain* (2004)

Harrison, B.H., *History of Oxford University in the 20th Century* (1997)

Harris, J., *William Beveridge: A Biography* (1997)

Hart, J., *Ask Me No More* (1998)

Little, I., *Little by Little* (2004)

Scott, D., *A D Lindsay: A Biography* (1971)

The College library holds papers of Norman Chester and Philip Williams to which access may be granted upon application to the Librarian.

College archives include records from David Fieldhouse, Max Hartwell, Ian Little and Vincent Wright, some of which may accessible with the permission of the Academic Administrator.

Index